Advance Praise for *Stand-Up Nation*

"In telling the largely hidden story of Israel's extraordinary outreach to the developing world, Aviva Klompas shows how tikkun olam is built into the identity of the Jewish state. Through a combination of idealism, empathy, and innovation, Israelis have shared their country's success story with those seeking to help their own countries grow. A compelling addition to the Israeli bookshelf."

—Yossi Klein Halevi, Author of
Letters to My Palestinian Neighbor

"At a time when Israel is wrapped in a cloak of grief and wrestles with existential fear for the future, those who love the Jewish state thirst for opportunities to be reminded of the miracle that Israel is and of the deep humanity that has shaped its soul. At precisely the right moment, Aviva Klompas provides a window into Israel that does just that. All of us who yearn to kindle our hope for the future are in her debt."

—Daniel Gordis, Author of *ISRAEL:*
A Concise History of a Nation Reborn

STAND-UP NATION

ISRAELI RESILIENCE IN THE WAKE OF DISASTER

AVIVA KLOMPAS

WS
WICKED SON

A WICKED SON BOOK
An Imprint of Post Hill Press
ISBN: 979-8-88845-432-9
ISBN (eBook): 979-8-88845-433-6

Stand-Up Nation:
Israeli Resilience in the Wake of Disaster

Cover Design by Jim Villaflores

This is a work of nonfiction. All people, locations, events, and situations are portrayed to the best of the author's memory.

Post Hill Press
New York • Nashville
wickedsonbooks.com
posthillpress.com

Published in the United States of America
1 2 3 4 5 6 7 8 9 10

With thanks to Dyonna Ginsburg, Yael Shapira, Hugo Gerstl, and Russell Robinson, each of whom kept answering the call to make this book possible.

עוד לא אבדה תקוותינו

Od lo avdah tikvatenu. Our hope is not yet lost.

TABLE OF CONTENTS

Letter from President Herzog

נשיא המדינה

رئيس الدولة

THE PRESIDENT

Jerusalem, March 19, 2024

Ms. Aviva Klompas

Dear Aviva,

I write to congratulate you on your upcoming book, "Stand Up Nation", which is being published at a truly critical time for our uniquely productive, and singularly afflicted, nation.

As always, context provides the most information. In May of 1948, just three years after the Allies won WWII, bringing an end to the greatest genocide in history- the Holocaust of the Jews, the Jewish, democratic State of Israel was born. Less than a decade later, in 1957, Israel's Foreign Ministry launched the official international development cooperation program, *Mashav*. Why would a young nation, threatened and isolated and barely getting by, proactively reach out to those less fortunate at such a delicate, challenging time?

Because that is precisely what Israel's founding fathers and mothers sought out to do in Israel's Declaration of Independence:

"We extend our hand ***to all neighboring states*** *and their peoples in an offer of peace and* ***good neighborliness****, and appeal to them to establish* ***bonds of cooperation and mutual help*** *with the sovereign Jewish people settled in its own land. The State of Israel is prepared* ***to do its share in a common effort*** *for the advancement of the entire Middle East.* "

The vision had been in place from the moment Israel was born. But the tenacity to realize it predated the state. This was the same tenacity that led survivors to Israel, the same resolve that enabled the Israeli people to overcome its enemies in the wars they waged, the same persistence that motivated the farmers of Be'eri and Nahal Oz to return to the crops and the fields, under fire. Indeed, it is the very same chutzpah, idealism, pragmatism & adventurism, as you so aptly write, that have built us as a nation.

I have every confidence that these are the attributes that will light our way forward, during these difficult times and in the better times I pray will soon come.

"Stand Up Nation" is an important contribution to our people's evolving story and I commend your impressive work.

Sincerely yours, and Shalom!

Isaac

Isaac Herzog

President of the State of Israel

FOREWORD

Dyonna Ginsburg, CEO of OLAM

It's been five months since the horrific Hamas attack on October 7. There's been a surge of anti-Israel sentiment and antisemitic incidents worldwide. The war in Gaza is still underway, and there's a threat of full-blown war with Hezbollah. Israeli civilians are still languishing in captivity, and tens of thousands of displaced Israelis are unable to return home.

Under such circumstances, it would be natural for Israelis to turn inward, focus exclusively on our own needs, and retreat from the outside world.

This book, however, offers another path. Written mostly before October 7, it lifts up the stories of Israelis, as well as people from developing countries who have spent time in Israel, who have chosen to step outside their own communities and serve others, often at personal risk. In so doing, it invites us to open our hearts and continue to engage with the wider world, even when it feels daunting and draining to do so.

Aviva Klompas and I met several years ago, in my capacity as CEO of OLAM, a network of Jewish and Israeli organizations working in the fields of international development, humanitarian aid, and global volunteering—including many of the nonprofits featured in this book. At the time, she was running study trips that showcased deep partnerships between Israeli organizations and communities living in low-income countries.

I quickly discovered that Aviva was not only a passionate champion of this work but also a history buff with an interest in the State of Israel's early years and the decision of its leaders to devote significant resources to bilateral aid, despite the fledgling state's numerous internal challenges.

Indeed, this book moves seamlessly between past and present, repeatedly alternating between Israel's pre-state and early years to contemporary stories of Israeli and Israeli-inspired nonprofits working in developing countries. At times, these shifts reveal a humanitarian commitment transmitted from generation to generation, as in the case of Eliyahu Saranga, who participated in Israel's first humanitarian mission in 1953, and his son, David, who responded to the recent earthquake in Turkey seventy years later; or Dr. Hillel Yaffe, who fought malaria in early twentieth-century Palestine, and his grandson, Professor Zvi Bentwich, who opened Israel's first AIDS clinic and works on eradicating neglected tropical diseases around the world.

In this way, this book conveys the powerful message that Israeli humanitarian aid and international development efforts are not historical anomalies. Neither are they a thin veneer atop the "real" Israel. Rather, they are intrinsic to Israeli identity, values, and ethos.

Each chapter can be read on its own, a stand-alone story perfect for bedside reading. But, in its entirety, this book presents a tapestry of Israelis engaged with the wider world, and people from around the world engaged with Israel, whose lives are interwoven in numerous ways.

In one chapter, we learn of Yossi Abramowitz's first day at the sun-scorched Kibbutz Ketura, which inspired him to found Israel's first solar field and eventually to build East Africa's first utility-scale solar field. Several chapters later, we discover that, at the very same kibbutz, Dr. Tareq Abu Hamed runs an environmental institute that has spearheaded clean water initiatives in Israel, Jordan, the West Bank, and Gaza, while also training students from across the African continent.

Through these stories, this book subtly challenges the binary between local and global, and internal and external needs. Rather than a zero-sum game, meeting internal and external needs is a virtuous cycle: local needs beget local solutions; local solutions inspire global interventions; global interventions succeed when tailored to the local context and implemented in deep partnership; insights gained in one location inform and improve the work in another.

As Aviva acknowledges herself, the topic of Israeli humanitarian work is often met with cynicism. On the right, people question its utility. On the left, they question its motives and legitimacy. In this sea of cynicism, this book tells the stories of real people—from Kenya, Indonesia, the Galilee, East Jerusalem, and elsewhere—trying to leave the world a bit better than how they found it. May their stories inspire us to do the same.

INTRODUCTION

"It's not enough to be up to date, you have to be up to tomorrow."

—David Ben-Gurion

I submitted the manuscript for this book in August 2023. Six weeks later, on October 7, Hamas and other terrorist organizations infiltrated Israel by land, air, and sea, and attacked nearby communities. Armed with RPGs, grenades, explosives, and automatic weapons, they brutally slaughtered 1200 people and took 253 hostages to Gaza.

The attack came almost fifty years to the day after Israel was taken by surprise in the 1973 Yom Kippur War. The thousands of terrorists who poured out of Gaza on October 7 infiltrated sleepy rural communities early on a Saturday morning on the dual Jewish holidays of Shabbat and Simchat Torah when families were still in their pajamas. They gunned down civilians in their homes, kidnapped mothers with babies in their arms, mutilated the bodies of men and women, and paraded captives through the streets of Gaza in a show of celebration. In a single day, Hamas slaughtered more Israelis than the total number murdered throughout the Second Intifada, which spanned five years.

The terrorists didn't care about religion or nationality. Their victims were Jews, Muslims, Christians, Buddhists, and Druze. They murdered thirty-nine foreign workers and abducted another twenty-four, most of whom worked in agriculture on kibbutzim near Gaza, where about 70 percent of the country's vegetables and 20 percent of its fruits are grown. Additionally, Hamas and other terrorists murdered thirteen students participating in MASHAV agricultural courses (ten from Nepal, two from Tanzania, one from Cambodia) and took many others hostage. As of the time of publication, one Nepali student and the body of a Tanzanian student remained in Hamas captivity.

Hamas has never played by the rules of war, but on October 7, they proved that they also don't play by the rules of civilization. October 7 saw the single-largest massacre of Jews since the Holocaust. The images that quickly spread round the world were reminiscent of the darkest period of Jewish history. Wearing GoPros and carrying cell phones, the terrorists filmed themselves ripping Jews from their homes, executing their victims in cold blood, and burning entire families alive. One survivor from Kibbutz Be'eri told me that all that he was missing was the numbers tattooed on his arm.

The country, and indeed Jewish communities all over the world, was gripped by grief and heartbreak. We grappled with a shattered sense of security and struggled to understand how an attack of this grotesque magnitude could have taken place inside the sovereign state of Israel with its military might, mythical intelligence, and feted technologies.

Most of the terrorists who perpetrated the attacks retreated to Gaza to hide behind the Palestinian civilian population. The terrorists knew Israel would be forced to respond, Palestinian civilians would get hurt, and the world would be outraged at

Israel. Sure enough, before Israel even began its ground invasion of Gaza, global sympathy for Israel had already morphed into outrage at Israel. Compounding the sense of betrayal were the tens of thousands of people who took to the streets to protest Israel even as the terrorists held hundreds of hostages.

No matter the evidence that emerged in the months that followed—that the terrorists had perpetrated sexual assault, that United Nations Relief and Works Agency (UNRWA) employees had participated in the massacre, that Hamas situated its headquarters under Gaza hospitals—global outrage remained fixed on Israel.

It wasn't the first time that Israel found itself isolated and fighting for its survival. The Jewish state was founded three years after the Holocaust that had decimated European Jewry. Its earliest days were beset by daunting economic and military hardships that gave Israel's leaders every reason to turn inward. Instead, they chose to engage with the world. In 1958, when Israel was itself still a struggling and impoverished developing country, it decided to establish an international development agency to reach out in friendship and support to other developing nations.

As with every previous crisis over the past seventy-five years, we must decide whether we are destined to be a people who dwells alone. In a world indifferent or even hostile to the fate of Jews, the natural inclination is to turn inward. Amidst the anguish and anger, we have long understood that we are the authors of our own story and ours is a story of human contribution. We are not meant to live in despair or accept injustice, and so we turn outward, determined to build a more connected, safer, prosperous, and compassionate world.

Two days after the October 7 attack that took the lives of one hundred community members, a handful of farmers returned to Kibbutz Be'eri to gather their cows and herd them back to safety. Soon after, farmers from Nahal Oz, a community situated just seven hundred meters from Gaza, sowed their crops under fire. Other kibbutzim bordering Gaza did the same even as the Israel Defense Forces (IDF) waged war against Hamas. So many of the farmers I met in the weeks that followed shared a resolve to work every square meter of their land right up to the border with Gaza.

I found a similar determination in the international development professional profiled in this book. Some were called to reserve duty while others joined in local volunteer efforts to assist survivors of October 7 and evacuees from communities threatened by Hamas and Hezbollah. They remained committed to a life of service. Some of them have added postscripts at the end of their chapters.

One of the people profiled in this book is Shoshan Haran from Kibbutz Be'eri. She and members of her family were abducted by terrorists on October 7, and her home was reduced to rubble. After enduring fifty days in Hamas captivity, sixty-seven-year-old Shoshan was released and returned to Israel alongside five of her family members: her daughter, Adi; her grandchildren Yahel (age three) and Neve (age eight); her sister-in-law Sharon Avigdori and Sharon's daughter, twelve-year-old Noam. Yahel and Naveh's father, Tal Shoham—Shoshan's son-in-law—remained in captivity. Back in Israel, Shoshan received the devastating news that her husband, Avshalom, and sister, Lilach, were murdered on October 7.

Shoshan is the founder of Fair Planet, which has enabled tens of thousands of previously impoverished African farmers to earn a good living while providing around one million people with a reliable source of food. A few weeks after her abduction, and before Shoshan was released, Fair Planet operations manager Alon Haberfeld sent a message to the team saying, "Shoshan, if she were here with us, would undoubtedly encourage us not to be deterred from her life's mission, ensuring access to adequate nutrition for the world's hungry. Her resounding message would echo in our hearts: 'Keep your focus on the bigger picture, keep supporting farmers in Africa.'"

On October 7, the communities surrounding Gaza became symbols of tragedy and destruction. As battered as they are, they are not broken and are already emerging as symbols of resilience and determination. October 7 will be recorded as one of the darkest days in Jewish history, but it will not be a day that defines us.

Israel's national anthem is called "Hatikva" and one particularly poignant line says: *Od lo avdah tikvateinu* (עוד לא אבדה תקותנו). It means Our Hope Is Not Yet Lost.

* * *

This book begins where my memoir, *Speaking for Israel,* left off. In it, I shared my experiences as the head speechwriter for Israel's delegation to the United Nations. The global body deals with a surprisingly wide-ranging array of topics—from peace and security to economics, human rights, natural resources, outer space, road safety, and the list goes on and on. The topic that most captured my imagination, however, was international development. While doing research for these speeches, I often fell down a rabbit hole reading about things I love: the stubborn tenacity of Jewish pioneers, ingenuity applied in the service of helping others, the trailblazing ways of Golda Meir, and most impressively, the story of how Israel as a fledgling developing nation turned to help other developing nations.

Following my time at the UN, I founded and led an initiative called Project Inspire to offer a glimpse into Israel's work in sustainable, social, economic, and environmental development in low-income nations. On study tours to Kenya, Uganda, India, Guatemala, and Nepal, we saw firsthand how local communities adopted Israeli know-how and technologies to combat poverty and address inequalities.

Traveling the world, I was often surprised to find signs of Israel in the most unlikely of places. While trekking in East Africa and walking through a small craft market, I spotted a handmade beaded bracelet with the flag of Israel alongside bracelets with the flags of Kenya, Tanzania, and Uganda. In the remote hills of Nepal, I happened upon a group of children, and as I passed by they yelled to me: "*Shalom! Namaste!* Hello!" In Uganda, I visited a remote island on Lake Victoria. Getting there required a windy bus ride, followed by a rickety boat ride, followed by another bumpy bus ride. When we finally reached Osanidde Village, an orphanage for children with HIV, we were greeted by teenagers who sang the Ugandan national anthem followed by "Hatikva," Israel's national anthem (not one member of the Jewish group that accompanied me was able to sing it by heart).

There were many more examples of finding Israel in the unlikeliest of places. Inevitably, if I inquired, I would discover stories of how Israelis had partnered in that community to save lives and improve the quality of life.

It still astounds me that little Israel has had such outsized impact in international development and humanitarian relief.

There are so many questions to answer. How did Israel, when it was itself a developing nation, manage to establish an international development agency? How did it find the capacity to help other nations even as it fought wars and battled economic hardships at home? How did tiny, impoverished Israel manage to gain expertise that would be sought after by countries worldwide? What has compelled so many Israelis to work in this field, and what have they managed to accomplish?

As this book reveals, Israel's distinct character and daunting challenges have uniquely positioned the Jewish state to contribute to solving pressing international development challenges. As Israel's first prime minister, David Ben-Gurion, said, "It's not enough to be up to date, you have to be up to tomorrow."

ISRAEL'S EARLY YEARS

"Independence came to us, as it was coming to Africa, not served up on a silver platter but after years of struggle."

—Golda Meir

Israel's early years were beset by unimaginable hardships. Enemies with large, well-funded armies waged wars of annihilation against the Jewish state. Even after ceasefires were professed, the border raids, shelling, and ambushes continued. On the world stage, the Jewish state faced social isolation from countries that refused to accept its existence for fear of earning the wrath of Arab nations. Waves of traumatized and penniless refugees from post-Holocaust Europe and Arab lands arrived with little more than the clothes on their backs and in need of substantial support to rebuild their lives. The dry and arid climate meant that water was in short supply and much of the country was unfarmable. The result was an economy on the verge of bankruptcy and a population struggling with critical shortages of essential goods, including food. People stood in line for hours to obtain basic goods, and an entire industry of substitute products emerged. Chicory tablets replaced coffee, bouillon cubes were used in place of chicken soup, and powdered eggs and milk replaced the real thing. People complained about spending hours a day in line, waiting for food.

For much of its first decade, Israel teetered from crisis to crisis. It faltered but never failed. Given the enormity of the challenges, it would have been reasonable for Israel's leaders to focus inward and address only the needs of their state and its citizens. Surprisingly though, it was during these early years of crises, when Israel was itself a developing nation, reliant on Jewish philanthropy and bilateral aid, that it established an international development agency called MASHAV (a Hebrew acronym for *HaMerkaz Le'Shituf Peulah Ben Leumi*), or "The Center for International Cooperation and Aid."

Founding an international development agency was hardly the norm in the late 1950s. MASHAV's founding predated the establishment of the United States Agency for International Development (USAID), the United Kingdom's Department for International Development (DFID), and the Canadian International Development Agency (CIDA). Israel barely had the funds to support its own citizens when it launched MASHAV; but its two champions, David Ben-Gurion, Israel's first prime minister, and Golda Meir, then Israel's foreign minister, pursued a dual mission. They believed that assisting other low-income nations was both a moral obligation and politically prudent.

In her autobiography, Golda Meir wrote, "We did what we did in Africa not because it was just a policy of enlightened self-interest—a matter of quid pro quo—but because it was a continuation of our own most valued traditions and an expression of our own deepest historic instincts."[1]

[1] Golda Meir, *My Life* (New York: G. P. Putnam's Sons, 1975), 319.

For his part, Ben-Gurion described Israel's support for emerging states as a "great historic privilege—which is therefore also a duty."[2] He explained, "And we Jews in our homeland must ask ourselves: Can Israel assist in the progress and development of Asia and Africa? For Israel, it is both a moral and a political issue, and from both aspects there is no doubt that Israel must look upon such aid as a historic mission, as necessary for Israel as it is beneficial to those we help."[3]

Ben-Gurion and Golda were keenly aware of realpolitik. Israel was surrounded by hostile neighbors in the Middle East and diplomatically isolated around the world. They hoped their efforts through MASHAV would earn some measure of support in the United Nations and friendship from the newly independent states of Africa and Asia. For a while, Israel became a global leader in supporting newly independent states. Precisely because it was small and poor, Israel had an advantage over larger, richer, and more established countries. It was a model and source of inspiration for newly emerging nations facing their own array of challenges. As Ben-Gurion wrote, "It is not because [Israel] is powerful and great, rich and generous, but because the new states regard her as a very suitable and instructive specimen of a country that is trying, with no little success, to solve problems that concern old and new in Asia and Africa."[4]

When it came to problem-solving, Israel was and is an unprecedented success story. Given the scope and scale of challenges, it has had no choice but to solve to survive.

---

[2] David Ben-Gurion, "Israel's Security and Her International Position Before and After the Sinai Campaign," *State of Israel Government Yearbook 5720* (Jerusalem: Israeli government, 1959–1960), 69.

[3] David Ben-Gurion, *Israel: Years of Challenge* (New York: Holt, Rinehart and Winston, 1963), 231.

[4] Ben-Gurion, "Israel's Security and Her International Position," 39.

"Whatever we attempt [in the state of the Jews] for our own benefit will redound mightily and beneficially to the good of all mankind."

—Theodor Herzl

In the early hours of November 30, 1947, a woman named Golda Meyerson stepped onto the balcony of the Jewish Agency building on Jerusalem's King George Street to address the jubilant crowds below. A short while earlier, the United Nations General Assembly had voted to divide British-administered Palestine into two independent states—one Arab and one Jewish. The decision as to whether there would be a Jewish state in the Jews' ancestral homeland had culminated in a four-minute roll call nearly six thousand miles away.

Days before, it had looked as though the resolution would fail. A two-thirds majority of members would need to vote in favor of passing the measure, and a preliminary head count revealed there wasn't enough support. Arab states stood firm against the establishment of a neighboring Jewish state, and other nations were reluctant to earn their fury. The General Assembly vote was scheduled for November 26, but more time was needed to convince countries to support the measure. Uruguay's representative to the UN launched a filibuster to delay the vote until after the Thanksgiving holiday. The Zionist coalition used the extra time to pursue every contact and avenue, ultimately convincing several foreign governments to change their vote. It helped that the two Cold War archrivals, the United States and the Soviet Union, were on the same side of the debate.

The historic vote took place Saturday night, November 29, 1947, at 5:35 New York time. Brazilian diplomat Oswaldo

Aranha presided over the meeting, and next to him sat the secretary general, Norwegian Trygve Lie. Jews around the world leaned close to radios as each country's delegate shouted from the floor, "Yes," "No," or "Abstention." Time seemed to stand still until the final tally was read aloud: "The resolution of the Ad Hoc Committee for Palestine was adopted by thirty-three votes in favor, thirteen opposed, and ten abstentions." The partition resolution dividing Palestine into sovereign Jewish and Arab states passed with the necessary two-thirds votes.

Celebrated Israeli novelist Amos Oz, in an autobiographical passage, recalled that night in Jerusalem when he was a boy and his father sat with him: "'From the moment we have our own state [said Oz's father], you will never be bullied just because you are a Jew and because Jews are so-and-sos. Not that. Never again. From tonight that's finished here. Forever.' I reached out sleepily to touch his face, just below his high forehead, and all of a sudden instead of his glasses my fingers met tears. Never in my life, before or after that night, not even when my mother died, did I see my father cry."[5]

It was 2:00 a.m. in Jerusalem when Golda arrived at the offices of the Jewish Agency. Hundreds of people had already gathered in the courtyard, some still wearing pajamas. They sang ecstatically, wept openly, and danced the hora, a lively Israeli circle dance. Golda stepped out onto the Jewish Agency balcony and, overcome with emotion, gathered herself to speak to the jubilant and teary crowd below. "For two thousand years we have waited for our deliverance. Now that it is here it is so great and wonderful that it surpasses human words. Jews," she

---

[5] Amos Oz, *A Tale of Love and Darkness* (Mariner Books, 2005) https://books.google.ca/books/about/A_Tale_of_Love_and_Darkness.html?id=4BF_QgAACAAJ&redir_esc=y

exclaimed, "*Mazel tov!*" She directed her words to the surrounding Arab nations and continued, "You have fought your battle against us in the United Nations. The partition plan is a compromise. Not what you wanted, not what we wanted. But now let us live in friendship and peace together."[6]

Below her, the crowd stopped dancing. People linked arms and sang "Hatikva." Throughout the night, Jerusalem reverberated with joy. People waved little blue and white flags, and stores handed out free bottles of wine to the joyous crowds.

That same evening, Golda warned that dreams came at a price. The United Nations was not handing the Jewish people a state, she cautioned. They would have to earn it with their lives. They would have to defend it from their enemies, and many lives would be lost. Israel's neighbors had made clear that if partition went ahead and a Jewish state was declared, there would be war. Hostilities had already been raging between Jews and Arabs under British-administered Palestine, and a broader regional war seemed likely. Several leaders of the *Yishuv* (the pre-state Jewish community) were fearful of pushing ahead with independence if it would mean starting a battle they couldn't win.

Six months after the partition vote in New York, ten men gathered in a second-floor meeting room in Tel Aviv to make the most significant decision confronting the Jewish people in two thousand years. The British would withdraw in two days. Time was running out for Yishuv leaders to decide whether to declare independence. Tensions ran high as the group debated the right course of action.

---

6 Francine Klagsbrun, *Lioness: Golda Meir and the Nation of Israel* (New York: Schocken Books, 2017), 292.

Leading the deliberations was David Ben-Gurion. Born David Green in Plonsk, a Polish city in the Russian Empire, in 1886, he grew up in a fervently Zionist family, attended the Hebrew school founded by his father, and immigrated to British-administered Palestine at the age of twenty. In a letter to his father, he described the excitement of his first night in the country, "I did not sleep. I was amid the rich smell of corn. I heard the braying of donkeys and the rustle of leaves in the orchards. Above were massed clusters of stars against the deep blue firmament. My heart overflowed with happiness."[7]

From the moment he stepped off the boat in Jaffa in 1906, the young man devoted himself to strengthening the Jewish presence in the country. He took the name Ben-Gurion ("son of a lion cub") after a first-century Jewish leader who rebelled against Roman rule. Ben-Gurion worked as a laborer building Jewish communities, then helped build political and labor parties. He published numerous articles in which he argued for Jewish self-sufficiency, the settlement of the land, and the importance of reviving the Hebrew language.

By 1948, Ben-Gurion was head of the Yishuv's provisional government. Military leaders predicted the chances of the Jews surviving against the combined forces of the Arab armies was fifty-fifty. The decision was agonizing. Declaring a state would almost certainly mean being invaded by Egypt, Transjordan, and Iraq, well-equipped militaries that had been armed and trained by the British over many years.

Would the Yishuv proclaim independence to realize the four-thousand-year-old vision of Jewish sovereignty in the Land

[7] Levi Soshuk and Azriel Louis Eisenberg, eds., *Momentous Century: Personal and Eyewitness Accounts of the Rise of the Jewish Homeland and State, 1875–1978* (Herzl Press, 1984), 71.

of Israel, knowing it could risk the lives of hundreds of thousands of Jews just three years after the Holocaust had decimated European Jewry? Could they allow statehood to slip through their fingers?

With time running out, the question was put to a vote. By a margin of six to four, the decision was made to declare a Jewish state. After centuries of persecution and pogroms, culminating in a genocide, it was time for Jews to take their own destiny into their own hands. Zionism, the national liberation movement of the Jewish people, was transformed from dream to reality. There would now be a place on earth where Jewish people would have the security and freedoms that come with sovereignty and self-determination.

Invitations for a declaration ceremony were quickly prepared. Jerusalem was under siege, so the ceremony would take place in Tel Aviv. The fortunate few who were invited to the most momentous occasion in two thousand years received a plain piece of folded printed paper delivered by bicycle courier. The text read:

> *We are honored to send to you this invitation to the Meeting of the Declaration of Independence, which will take place on Thursday, the 5th of Iyar 5708 (May 14, 1948) at four o'clock in the afternoon in the auditorium of the Museum (Rothschild Boulevard 16).*

A final note said, *"Dress code: dark holiday clothing."* The invitation asked invitees to keep secret the details and the time of the meeting. Yishuv leaders feared that if word got out, the ceremony would become the target of an attack. Unsurprisingly, word did get out, and hundreds of excited people gathered outside the Tel Aviv Museum on leafy Rothschild Boulevard to be present at the birth of the Jewish state.

Early in the afternoon of May 14, Ben-Gurion presented the final draft of the Declaration of Independence for approval by the People's Council, the precursor of the Knesset (Israel's parliament). At four o'clock in the afternoon, with cameras rolling and people all over the world listening, Ben-Gurion rapped his gavel from a hastily erected stage in the museum's main hall. The attendees rose and unprompted sang "Hatikva," the anthem of the Zionist movement. Its words "To be a free people in our homeland" must have struck a chord deep in their hearts as they prepared to witness the Jewish dream become a reality.

Ben-Gurion stood in front of a portrait of Theodor Herzl, which hung between floor-to-ceiling flags bearing the Star of David, and read the declaration, which began:

"The Land of Israel was the birthplace of the Jewish people. Here their spiritual, religious and political identity was shaped. Here they first attained statehood, created cultural values of national and universal significance and gave to the world the eternal Book of Books." It continued with the promise, "The State of Israel will be open for Jewish immigration and for the Ingathering of the Exiles."

When Ben-Gurion finished reading the declaration, the *Shehecheyanu* prayer was recited, a Jewish prayer of gratitude. "Hatikva" was performed once again, this time accompanied by the Jewish Philharmonic Orchestra. After which, Ben-Gurion proclaimed, "The State of Israel has arisen. The meeting is ended." The dream of a Jewish homeland was born, but there was little time to celebrate. Ben-Gurion wrote in his diary that day, "At four o'clock in the afternoon Jewish independence was declared and the State of Israel was established. Its destiny is now in the hands of our defense forces."[8]

At midnight the British High Commissioner left, and the first shots were fired in Israel's War of Independence. To the Arab world, the "*Nakba*" (Arabic for catastrophe) had materialized. Arab armies launched a bloody assault against Jewish armed forces that were sorely ill-equipped and desperately underfunded.

While fighting for its survival, newborn Israel braced for a massive wave of immigrants. Ben-Gurion set aliyah (immigration to Israel) and absorption as one of the country's top priorities. On the day it was founded, Israel had 806,000 citizens. By the time the War of Independence ended thirteen months later, another 340,000 immigrants had arrived. Israel's population doubled in the first two years of its existence. Over the next seven years, the country grew by another third. Any country would be overwhelmed by this rate of population growth. Most of the new arrivals were impoverished refugees escaping persecution. This first wave included Holocaust survivors, some from displaced persons camps in Germany, Austria, and Italy, and others from British detention camps in Cyprus.

Not long afterward, hundreds of thousands of penniless Jews from the surrounding Muslim countries in Asia and Africa poured into Israel. Humiliated at their failure to snuff out Israel, Arab governments and Iran turned their fury on their Jewish populations. Across the Arab world, Jewish-owned businesses and properties were confiscated. Homes were burned to the ground. Synagogues were looted, graveyards desecrated, and scores of Jews were murdered. Within a few years, Jewish communities that had existed in the Middle East for more than

[8] Ben-Gurion, *Israel: Years of Challenge*, 43.

2,500 years were destroyed and most of the Arab world's Jewish population had fled. Of the 850,000 Jewish refugees who fled, nearly 600,000 resettled in Israel. The state welcomed these newcomers even as its leaders struggled to meet the vast needs of the burgeoning population.

The demands of financing a war of survival, defending against constant existential threats, and providing for the needs of a rapidly growing population pushed the new nation to the brink of financial collapse. The stress on Israel's fledgling economy was further strained by an Arab economic boycott that caused oil costs to rise. In early 1949, Israel's first elected government prepared to institute an austerity system to cope with the dire economic situation. It set up ma'abarot, temporary absorption camps, because there simply wasn't enough housing for the hundreds of thousands of new arrivals. Ben-Gurion described them as "far from satisfactory, but the best we could do at the time."[9] Families lived in tiny shacks made from tin or wood without running water or electricity. Water could be retrieved from central faucets but had to be boiled before drinking. The public showers and lavatories were usually inadequate and in disrepair.

The economic crisis persisted. The state had almost no money to provide food, medical care, schooling, job training, and other basic needs. Despite the challenges, Israel continued to welcome waves of new immigrants. Conditions grew so difficult that the government instituted severe rationing measures called *tzena* (based on the Hebrew word for "modesty") for a decade. In 1949, a statement read before the Knesset, Israel's 120-member parliament, outlined a plan to ration food, clothing, and all essential provisions. To oversee the process, Israel

---

[9] Ben-Gurion, *Israel: Years of Challenge*, 58.

established a Ministry of Rationing and Provision. Lacking food and foreign currency, the government imposed a strict food ration of 1,600 calories per person a day. The ministry created a "basket" of products with basics such as sugar, oil, bread, and margarine, which could only be purchased in authorized stores. Each family was given a coupon book that worked on a points system, which determined the type and amount of food and clothes to be obtained. There were so many points for meat, so many for powdered eggs and dried milk, and so on. People were permitted 360 grams of bread per day, 60 grams of corn flour, 60 grams of white flour, 17 grams of rice, 58 grams of sugar, and a monthly allowance of 750 grams of meat, 200 grams of cheese, 12 eggs, and 3.5 kilos of potatoes.[10]

Everything was hard to come by. Agricultural fields lay bare, and imports were limited. Two thirds of Israel's land was arid or semiarid, and much of the soil was of poor quality. The pioneering Zionists who arrived in British-administered Palestine did not find a land of milk and honey as depicted in the Bible. They found blazing sand dunes along the coast, swampy malaria-riddled plains, rocky hills in the east, and a south that was unbearably hot in summer. The first decade of Israel's existence was plagued by security and economic and social hardships, any one of which was enough to snuff out a newborn nation. Yet it persisted, facing down each challenge one by one.

---

[10] Daniel Gordis, *Impossible Takes Longer* (New York: HarperCollins, 2023), 183.

"The difficult we do immediately.
The impossible takes a little longer."
—David Ben-Gurion

Fighting for survival meant fighting wars on the one hand and finding ways to build an economy that could support its citizens on the other. In the 1950s, the standard of living for the average Israeli was comparable to that of Americans in the 1800s.[11] Israel's founders believed it was critical for the state to achieve agricultural self-reliance, a seemingly impossible task in land with scarce precipitation and lacking natural water resources. From the southernmost tip of the Negev Desert to the northern border with Lebanon, only 18 percent of Israel's twenty-two-thousand-square-kilometer landmass is arable. Ben-Gurion was a farmer, and so were half of his cabinet members. They saw agriculture as a national mission, and so through the 1950s and 1960s, the government spent approximately a third of the national budget on agriculture and water infrastructure. An additional 30 percent was spent on education and another 30 percent on security.[12]

To fund this mission, Israel appealed to diaspora Jews for support, and they responded generously. In 1948 alone, they sent nearly $147 million to Israel to keep the struggling nation afloat.[13] In the ensuing years, Ben-Gurion pushed ahead with a controversial agreement to accept reparation payments from

---

11 Dan Senor and Saul Singer, *Start-up Nation: The Story of Israel's Economic Miracle* (New York: Twelve, 2011), 15.

12 Danielle Abraham, Thierry Ngoga, Jonathan Said, and Merav Yachin, *How Israel Became a World Leader in Agriculture and Water* (London: Tony Blair Institute for Global Change, September 2019), 20.

13 Jewish Virtual Library, "American Jewish Contributions to Israel," https://www.jewishvirtuallibrary.org/american-jewish-contributions-to-israel.

Germany. There was bitter debate in Israel over whether to accept the money, with Ben-Gurion reluctantly but firmly in favor, and right-wing Knesset backbencher Menachem Begin vehemently opposed. The notion of accepting "blood money" from Germany outraged many Jews, particularly those whose family members had been murdered in the Holocaust. Despite the outrage, Ben-Gurion remained stubbornly focused on ensuring the survival of living Jews in barely solvent Israel. He made clear that reparations were not meant to put a "price" on the lives lost but would be regarded as material compensation for property stolen and livelihoods cut short.

Reparation funds were used to improve housing, roads, electricity networks, and build critical national infrastructure, including Israel's National Water Carrier project. Ben-Gurion oversaw plans to develop this large-scale water project, which would transport water from the Sea of Galilee to the Negev Desert in the south, a distance of 250 kilometers. It was a feat of imagination and daring, requiring entire innovations in engineering.

Policies were implemented to subsidize water for agricultural needs, and experts were dispatched by the Agriculture Ministry to disseminate new agricultural methods. At the same time, the government funded agricultural research and established R&D centers to develop new techniques for farming in arid conditions. This effort built on the work of Yitzhak Elazari Volcani, who came to British-administered Palestine in 1908 and established an agricultural research station. It grew into today's Agricultural Research Organization, located at the Volcani Center, south of Tel Aviv. Over the years, the learnings were broadly shared with farmers via trainers called extension workers. Following years of focused investment in agriculture and education, Israel transformed areas of the desert into flourishing agricultural lands, achieved the goal of agricultural self-sufficiency, and became an exporter of agricultural produce. An April 1960 issue of *Scientific American* described the twelve-year-old country as follows:

> It had more than doubled its cultivated land, to a million acres. It had drained 44,000 acres of marshland and extended irrigation to 325,000 acres; it had increased many-fold the supply of underground water from wells and was far along on the work of diverting and utilizing the scant surface waters. On vast stretches of uncultivable land it had established new range-cover to support a growing livestock industry and planted 37 million trees in new forests and shelter belts. All this had been accomplished under a national plan that enlisted the devotion of the citizens and the best understanding and technique provided by modern agricultural science.[14]

Today, more than 40 percent of Israel's vegetables and crops are grown in the desert. A once nearly uninhabitable region is now home to fish farms, olive groves, date orchards, and vineyards. A vast assortment of fruits and vegetables blossom from arid land, even though annual rainfall totals are measured in inches and the proximity to the Dead Sea means the groundwater is highly saline. Out of necessity, Israel became a world

[14] Walter C. Lowdermilk, "50 Years Ago: The Reclamation of a Man-Made Desert," *Scientific American* (April 1960), https://www.scientificamerican.com/article/reclamation-of-man-made-desert/.

leader in water management. Desalinated water provides as much as 85 percent of water for domestic and industrial uses, and Israel treats 93 percent of its wastewater, allowing it to be reused for agricultural purposes.

Even before Israel became an economic and agricultural success story, it was finding ways to support other low-income countries. Absent material wealth, Israel couldn't offer sizable grants or loans, like larger, more prosperous states. Instead, it shared what it did have: knowledge and partnership. It offered human aid in the form of specialists who could advise on everything from agriculture to infrastructure. As Ben-Gurion wrote, "Some doubt whether it is in Israel's reach to render a sizable measure of help. She is still, and for years will be, herself in need of aid from world Jewry and support from her friends abroad. No other country has such serious problems of security.... What then, can Israel contribute to the new countries in Asia and Africa and how? The simple and truthful answer is by what she does for herself in her own country."[15]

"Fan the tiny inner spark of possibility
into flames of achievement."

—Golda Meir

The driving force behind Israel's international development program was Golda Meir. Bold, brash, flawed, sarcastic, eloquent, staunchly Zionist, and a determined feminist ahead of her time, Golda Meir is my answer to the question, "Which

[15] David Ben-Gurion, "Towards a New World," in *The Role of the Israel Labour Movement in Establishing Relations with States in Africa and Asia–Documents* (Jerusalem: Hebrew University, 1989, originally published 1960), 38.

historic figure would you invite to a dinner party?" Known for speaking her mind with forthright candor, Golda was a formidable woman who captivated kings and presidents with her sharp mind and dry wit, while her unpretentious character and practical outlook endeared her to ordinary people all over the world.

In 1969, she became Israel's fourth prime minister and the first female world leader to earn the role without inheriting it from a father or husband. *Time* magazine's September 1969 cover depicts Golda as she was: a stern and frumpy woman with wispy gray and white hair that refused to be tamed in a knot. Other photographs show the global icon in coarsely cut tweed suits, clunky purse in hand, standing in practical, boxy orthopedic shoes. She wore no makeup, smoked like a chimney, and entertained foreign dignitaries in her official ministry apartment, serving home-cooked meals that she herself prepared. The kitchen of her small apartment hummed with the sound of coffee brewing from two kettles on the gas stovetop.

Unpretentious as she was, Golda was a global superstar. When Gallup ran its annual poll in 1971 asking American women which woman in the world they admired most, Golda won, becoming just the second woman from outside the United States to top the list. She repeated this achievement in 1973, earning more than twice as many votes as Pat Nixon, and again in 1974, beating out Betty Ford. Simply put, Golda was a sensation, and she earned this distinction for her service to the State of Israel.

One would hardly expect all this given her humble start in life. Born to a Jewish family in Kiev, Ukraine, in 1898, Golda began life as Goldie Mabovitch. She was named after her maternal great-grandmother, a domineering matriarch who lived to be ninety-four and who put salt instead of sugar in her tea to remember the bitterness of the Jewish exile. Golda's early childhood was marked by extreme poverty and traumatic anti-Semitic pogroms at the hands of the Cossacks. When she was eight years old, her family escaped to the United States and settled in Milwaukee, Wisconsin, where her father worked as a railroad carpenter and her mother ran a grocery.

Even as a child, Golda knew her own mind. She was active in the Zionist youth movement and lobbied her parents to let her attend high school so she could pursue a career. Fed up with the refrain that "men don't like smart girls," she snuck away to Denver to live with her married sister, who regularly hosted intellectual evenings at her home. There, she was exposed to vivid debates on Zionism, women's suffrage, trade unionism, literature, and music. A regular attendee at these evenings was a man named Morris Meyerson. The two eventually married and, at Golda's insistence, moved to Palestine. The couple settled on Kibbutz Merhavia.

Golda reveled in the hard work and embraced opportunities to contribute to kibbutz life. Morris, on the other hand, was miserable. He was never able to transform from a bookish lover of poetry to an idealistic laborer. He hated the kibbutz's communal way of life and grew increasingly unhappy and withdrawn. It didn't help that he also contracted malaria. Seeing the tormenting effect that kibbutz life had on him, Golda finally relented, and the couple relocated to Jerusalem, where Golda gave birth to a son named Menachem and later a daughter named Sarah. It was a difficult time in British-administered Palestine, and the young family endured grinding poverty. In exchange for the children's nursery school fees, Golda agreed to wash the school's laundry by hand. At home, they struggled to heat their apartment in winter and were so in debt to the local grocer that he refused to extend any more credit.

In 1928, at the age of thirty, the trajectory of Golda's life changed when she was offered a job on the secretariat of the Women Workers' Council. She knew Morris wouldn't approve but accepted the job anyway. Ignoring his objections, Golda relocated to Tel Aviv with the children and without Morris. Clever and determined, she was well suited to the work and moved quickly up the organizational ranks, becoming a member of the Executive Committee of the Histadrut (General Organization of Workers) in 1934 and head of its political department two years later. During World War II, she held several key posts in the World Zionist Organization and in the Jewish Agency, which functioned as a sort of de facto government for the Jews of Palestine.

By 1946, most of the Jewish leadership had been arrested by the British authorities for smuggling in Jewish refugees or for activities of the Haganah (the underground military organization of the Yishuv), including Moshe Sharett, head of the political department of the Jewish Agency. Golda became acting head of the Jewish Agency, where she proved herself a forceful spokesperson on behalf of Jewish refugees and lobbied hard for the release of her Zionist colleagues.

Golda's commitment to the Zionist cause was rewarded when, at the age of fifty, she became one of the signatories of Israel's Declaration of Independence. A month after the state's founding, she was appointed Israel's first ambassador to the Soviet Union and given the first passport issued by the newborn Jewish state.

In her memoir, Golda writes:

> A story—which, as far as I know, is all it was—once went around that Ben-Gurion described me as the "only man" in his cabinet. What amused me about it was that obviously he (or whoever invented the story) thought this was the greatest possible compliment that could be paid to a woman. I very much doubt that any man would have been flattered if I had said about him that he was the only woman in the government![16]

In 1949, Golda was elected to the Knesset and appointed by Prime Minister Ben-Gurion to be the minister of labor, responsible for immigrant settlement, housing, job creation, and transportation. This included the herculean task of finding jobs and housing for the nearly seven hundred thousand new immigrants. She tackled soaring unemployment by enacting social welfare policies, providing subsidized housing for immigrants, and coordinating their integration into the workforce.

There continued to be an influx of poverty-stricken, homeless Jews from the displaced persons camps of Europe and the ghettos of Arabic-speaking countries. To feed the growing population, the state had to import food, but it was chronically on the verge of bankruptcy. The British had frozen their pounds sterling, and there was no foreign currency to buy foreign produce.[17] Local agriculture only provided about 15 percent of the population's food requirements. Wheat had to be imported as

---

16 Meir, *My Life*, 108.

17 Moshe Sharett to Walter Eytan, September 3, 1952, in Yehoshua Freundlich, ed., *Documents on the Foreign Policy of Israel* (Jerusalem: Israel State Archive, 1992), 7: 485–88. https://www.un.org/unispal/document/auto-insert-210827/

did meat, fish, and the grains necessary to feed livestock. People stood in line for hours to obtain goods. Golda traveled to the United States repeatedly to beg American Jews for financial support. With her trademark stoic pragmatism, she detailed the hardships Israel faced and would present the choices as follows: either give in or grit their teeth and fight on as many fronts as necessary for as long as necessary.

"I am prouder of Israel's international cooperation program and of the technical aid we gave to the people of Africa than I am of any other single project we have ever undertaken."

—Golda Meir

Golda held the Labor portfolio for seven years. She would have liked to remain in the role, but in 1956 Ben-Gurion made her foreign minister, the second-highest position in the government. Her appointment catapulted her onto the world stage. Perhaps because of this outward focus, Ben-Gurion insisted she adopt a Hebrew-sounding surname, and so Myerson became Meir.

Newly responsible for representing the country's affairs, Golda took stock of the situation. Israel was tiny, fledgling, and poor. A small Jewish island in the predominantly Muslim Middle East, Israel was surrounded by neighbors who viewed it as illegitimate. In the United Nations, it was disliked and misunderstood by most delegates. Golda saw it as her mission to make friends in the global community. In the newborn nations of Africa, she saw opportunity.

When Ghana gained independence in 1957, Israel sent a Vienna-born diplomat named Ehud Avriel to serve as its ambassador to Ghana, Congo (from 1960 to 1966, the country was also known as Congo-Léopoldville), and Liberia. Avriel encouraged Golda to attend the first anniversary of Ghana's independence and take the opportunity to visit neighboring Côte d'Ivoire, Liberia, Senegal, and Nigeria. The five-week tour would be the start of a charm offensive across the African continent. African states accounted for about one-quarter of the United Nations membership, and Israel desperately needed friendships and alliances.

Golda's first stop was Monrovia, capital of Liberia, where she was warmly greeted by President William Tubman. He recounted that during a visit to Washington over a decade earlier, Tubman had been questioned by a congressional committee on working conditions in Liberia. Finding his answers unsatisfying, the United States temporarily cut ties with his country. Emanuel Celler, a Jewish congressman, befriended the African leader and helped him present his case once more to Congress. Grateful for this kindness, Tubman instructed his United Nations delegation to vote in favor of partition in 1947, paving the way for the establishment of Israel. Thanks to Congressman Celler, Tubman remained a lifelong friend of the Jews and of the State of Israel.

From Liberia, Golda continued to Ghana, sub-Saharan Africa's first decolonized independent state. As part of its independence celebration, Ghana hosted the First All-African People's Congress, which included a gathering of national liberation movement leaders across the continent. When Golda entered the conference room, she found herself in front of an enormous table, around which sat representatives of nations striving for independence. Her arrival provoked noticeable friction in the room. The representative from Algeria rose and demanded to know how Israel could be purchasing arms from

France, a country that sought to undermine African self-determination. Finding her seat, Golda took in the tense scene and lit a cigarette. Ignoring the cold stares, she calmly explained, "Our neighbors are out to destroy us with arms they receive free of charge from the Soviet Union and for very little money from other sources. The one and only country in the world that is ready—for hard currency, and a lot of it—to sell us some of the arms we need in order to protect ourselves is France."[18] Not waiting for a reply, she described in detail on Israel's predicament before bluntly concluding, "If de Gaulle were the devil himself, I would regard it as the duty of my government to buy arms from the only source available to us. And now let me ask you a question. If you were in that position, what would you do?"[19] Golda's unapologetic candor earned her the respect of the delegates, and soon conversation turned to questions of state building.

If the African tour was a great success, Golda was a sensation. Women, in particular, loved her. At one gathering, she was clothed in traditional robes and crowned a paramount chief, an honor rarely bestowed on women. Traveling across the continent, Golda was equally comfortable with dignitaries and regular citizens and often invited both to join her in dancing the hora. A good sport, she accepted an invitation to try the highlife, a popular West African dance, much to the delight of her hosts.

Golda immersed herself in getting to know Africa's newest nations. She saw how their struggles for independence and their desire to provide for their people mirrored the struggles Israel had faced. When she returned home, she embarked on a

---

18 Klagsbrun, *Lioness*, 438.

19 Meir, *My Life*, 314.

mission to see Israel formally share its knowledge and experience in infrastructure, health, education, and agriculture. She convinced Ben-Gurion that Israel should launch an official development cooperation program as a division within its Ministry of Foreign Affairs. In 1960, the section became an independent department called the Department for International Assistance and Cooperation, whose name was later changed to MASHAV, a Hebrew acronym referring to The Center for International Cooperation and Aid.

Before long, MASHAV was dispatching technical experts around the world. During MASHAV's first year of operations, 137 course participants arrived in Israel and 80 Israeli experts were sent abroad. By 1963, there were 1,263 trainees coming from Africa, Asia, the Middle East, and Latin America. Training courses were held in ten countries and attended by nearly 400 trainees. Between 1958 and 1971, 4,341 experts served MASHAV, 2,763 of whom were sent to the African continent. Globally there were 15,258 course participants, 6,797 of them from African countries.[20]

At times, Israeli diplomats or members of the Knesset asked that international assistance be conditioned on political support. The suggestion was repeatedly rejected, including by Abba Eban, who served as Israel's foreign minister from 1966–1974. He was adamant that the act of giving had value in its own right and it was not to be conditioned.[21]

As African states achieved independence, Israel was often one of the first nations to extend a hand of friendship, sending ambassadors to serve in thirty-three countries through the

---

20 Shimeon Amir, *Israel's Development Cooperation with Africa, Asia and Latin America* (New York: Praeger Publishers, 1974), 94, 97, 98.

21 Arye Oded, "Fifty Years of MASHAV Activity," *Jewish Political Studies Review* (Fall 2009), https://jcpa.org/article/fifty-years-of-mashav-activity/.

1950s and 1960s.[22] As a result, Israel had more embassies in Africa than any other country besides the United States. When asked why Israel was so focused on the African continent, Golda explained:

> Independence came to us, as it was coming to Africa, not served up on a silver platter, but after years of struggle. Like those nations, we had to shake off foreign rule; like them, we had to learn for ourselves how to reclaim the land, how to increase the yields of our crops, how to irrigate, how to raise poultry, how to live together and how to defend ourselves.... We have been forced to find solutions to problems that large, wealthy, powerful states had never encountered.[23]

From the perspective of many African nations, Israel was a natural partner. It had successfully freed itself of British rule, opened its doors to settle new refugees, and navigated the complicated work of state-building. Newly independent nations wanted to learn how Israel was harnessing agriculture to provide food sustainability for a growing population, industrializing its economy, and building centers of education and health care. Israel was happy to share its knowledge, experience, and pioneering spirit of innovation.

---

[22] Remarks by Dr. Peter Pham, Vice President for Research and Regional Initiatives, Director, Africa Center, Atlantic Council, "Celebrating the 60th Anniversary of MASHAV," YouTube, https://www.youtube.com/watch?v=heeF598ZZJw (timestamp 1:13).

[23] Meir, *My Life*, 318.

Through MASHAV, Israel helped establish and run Ghana's Black Star shipping line, which reduced the cost of exporting cacao and importing manufactured goods.[24] Israel's water planning authority, Tahal, assisted with water infrastructure development, while the Ghana National Construction Company was established with help from Israeli construction firm Solel Boneh. In Mali, MASHAV helped develop a fish-processing program, while in Tanzania it partnered on a youth leadership training center. Israeli experts helped Nigerians build their house of parliament, and many main roads and bridges. In the Ivory Coast and Sierra Leone, they developed potable water projects, and in Uganda they paved the road to the Rwandan border. When Congo faced a critical shortage of physicians, Patrice Lumumba, the first prime minister of the Congo, and Dag Hammarskjöld, secretary-general of the United Nations, turned to Israel for assistance. Golda mobilized the Israeli army medical corps to send a team of forty-eight physicians and nurses.

As foreign minister, Golda logged more than one hundred thousand miles on trips through the African continent. In her memoir, she writes about "spending hours doing things that I had never in my wildest dreams expected to do, such as presiding over the election of a beauty queen during Independence Day festivities of Cameroun, or going out to dinner in Abidjan, on the Ivory Coast, with a group of African leaders and hearing an African band strike up a stirring rendition of 'Die Yiddishe Mama' as soon as I walked in."[25]

In 1964, she attended the Independence Day ceremonies of Zambia alongside the country's president, the prime minister of Kenya, the president of Tanzania, and the president of

---

[24] Klagsbrun, *Lioness*, 438.

[25] Meir, *My Life*, 316.

Senegal. A VIP visit was arranged for foreign dignitaries to visit the famous Victoria Falls, which spanned Zambia and what was then known as South Rhodesia (today Zimbabwe). When the group's buses arrived at the border, Rhodesian police officers refused to let the Black dignitaries step off the bus, even though they were personal guests of Zambian President Kaunda. Appalled, Golda refused to leave the bus saying, "I have no intention of being separated from my friends." The bus turned around and returned to Lusaka, where Golda writes, "President Kaunda received me as though I were Joan of Arc rather than just a woman who couldn't and wouldn't tolerate racial discrimination in any form."[26]

Following another trip, American evangelist Billy Graham asked Golda how she had come to be such a popular figure on the continent. She replied, "Maybe it's because we go there to teach, not to preach."[27] Teaching was at the heart of Israel's development efforts. Golda helped organize a seminar in Haifa titled "The Role of Women in a Developing Society," which brought together delegates from twenty-two African and Asian nations. "The world will not know peace, and there will be no real happiness until we, the new peoples of the world, reach a standard of living and education that is comparable to that of the older-established and wealthier nations," she said. "And since the problems are so great, fifty percent of the people—the male population by itself—cannot solve it."

This seminar laid the foundation for the creation of the International Training Centre in Haifa, which was later renamed the Golda Meir Mount Carmel International Training Center. Since 1960, it has provided seminars for people from

[26] Meir, *My Life*, 324.

[27] Klagsbrun, *Lioness*, 441.

Asia, Africa, and Latin America in Sustainable Community Development, Entrepreneurship and Innovation, and Early Childhood Education, all with gender equality as a cross-cutting issue. The facility was established almost fifteen years before the UN held its first world conference on women, where it set out guidelines for the advancement of women.

A decade after its establishment, MASHAV had trained more than ten thousand Africans, Asians, and Latin Americans from more than ninety countries and dispatched more than four thousand Israeli experts to sixty-two countries.[28] They set up demonstration farms, taught business courses, and helped design irrigation and drinking water systems. At the same time, hundreds of Africans were invited to Israel to attend specialized courses. The Hebrew University-Hadassah Medical School trained African health-care professionals, while the Technion (Israel Institute of Technology) taught a generation of engineers. By 1964, the Israeli ratio of international development experts to total population was twice that of the international Organization for Economic Cooperation and Development (OECD) average, and second only to France.[29] By the end of the 1960s, Israel's bilateral aid budget, while small in absolute terms, was comparable to that of the world's largest and most developed countries, as a percentage of its gross domestic product (GDP).[30]

---

[28] Aliza Belman Inbal and Shachar Zahavi, *The Rise and Fall of Israel's Bilateral Aid Budget, 1958–2008* (Tel Aviv University, Harold Hartog School of Government and Policy, 2009), 16, https://pearsfoundation.org.uk/wp-content/uploads/2018/06/riseandfall.pdf.

[29] Joel Peters, *Israel and Africa: The Problematic Friendship* (London: British Academic Press, 1992), 4.

[30] Inbal and Zahavi, *The Rise and Fall of Israel's Bilateral Aid Budget,* 11.

Israel had become a leader in international development, and its model was praised by both the UN Development Program (UNDP) and the OECD's Development Assistance Committee in the 1960s and early 1970s. As one UN official said, "The study of Israel's unique efforts and achievements in the field of economic development...provides the curious visitor with more useful hints for the solution of problems in under-developed economies than any other country known to me."[31] At its height, MASHAV was the largest department in Israel's Ministry of Foreign Affairs, and Israel had, per capita, one of the most extensive technical assistance programs in the Western world.[32]

The friendships and partnerships forged during MASHAV's first decade soon gave way to realpolitik. The 1967 Six-Day War set in motion an alarming deterioration in relations between Israel and African nations. For years, there had been clashes between Israel and its Arab neighbors. Egyptian and Syrian leaders repeatedly declared that war was imminent, and their goal was to wipe Israel off the map. Events escalated when, in May 1967, Egyptian President Gamal Abdel Nasser expelled UN peacekeepers from the Sinai Peninsula, blocked Israeli shipping lanes in the Red Sea, and mobilized the Egyptian military. Israel launched preemptive air strikes that crippled the air forces of Egypt and its allies. The brief war ended with a UN-brokered ceasefire, but it significantly altered the map of the Mideast. Israel had captured the Jordanian West Bank, the Syrian Golan Heights, and Egypt's Sinai Peninsula and Gaza Strip. By

---

31 Mordechai E. Kreinin, *Israel and Africa: A Study in Technical Cooperation* (New York: F. A. Praeger, 1964), 11.

32 Moshe Decter, *To Serve, To Teach, To Leave: The Story of Israel's Development Assistance Program in Black Africa* (New York: New York American Jewish Congress, 1977), 8.

capturing Sinai—territory that had belonged to Egypt, a member of the Organization of African Unity—lines were drawn. There was an expectation that African countries would stand in solidarity with Egypt, their "African sister."

The events of 1967 provided Arab nations with ammunition to convince African leaders that Israel was acting as a colonial entity. Pro-Arab sentiment was growing in Africa, in part because of the decision taken by oil-rich Arab nations to pledge lavish aid packages to the continent.

At the September 1973 conference of the Non-Aligned Movement, a resolution was adopted to affirm the legitimacy of the Palestinians struggle against "colonialism," while also expressing "concern at Israel's policy of aggression and expansion." The resolution called for member countries to boycott Israel economically, diplomatically, militarily, and culturally.

A surprise attack from Egypt and Syria one month later on Yom Kippur caught Israel unaware, and it barely eked out a victory that cost the lives of twenty-six hundred soldiers in three weeks of desperate fighting. Israeli forces pushed the attacking Egyptian forces back over the Suez Canal, but within a couple of months, African nations began to cut diplomatic ties with Israel.[33] Abba Eban, then foreign minister, described their decision as a "gross betrayal of international friendship and goodwill."[34] The feeling of treachery was echoed throughout Israeli society, which had been intensely proud of its development cooperation until countries began turning their back on Israel.

---

[33] Zach Levey, "Israel's Exit from Africa, 1973: The Road to Diplomatic Isolation," *British Journal of Middle Eastern Studies* 35, no. 2 (August 2008): 208, https://cris.haifa.ac.il/en/publications/israels-exit-from-africa-1973-the-road-to-diplomatic-isolation.

[34] Inbal and Zahavi, "The Rise and Fall of Israel's Bilateral Aid Budget," 41.

Relations continued to worsen. Libya's Muammar Gaddafi, then head of the Organization of African States, pressured sub-Saharan African nations to sever their ties with the Jewish state and align with the Arab League boycott. African countries that kept their relations with Israel were threatened with increased oil prices. Thirty African countries succumbed to the economic pressure and cut formal ties with Israel. Only Malawi, Lesotho, and Swaziland retained full diplomatic relations.[35]

At the same time, the Yom Kippur War plummeted Israel into economic disaster. Most of the country's labor force was called into military service, leaving businesses unable to function. Government policies that artificially propped up salaries led to ballooning public debt. To offset the growing debt, taxes were hiked. The consequences were dire, leading to a devaluing of the local currency by 43 percent. Hyperinflation hit in the early 1980s and in 1984 reached 445 percent.[36] A trip to the supermarket meant spending thousands of near worthless shekels.

The low point in Israeli-African relations came in November 1975, when nineteen African countries voted in favor of the infamous United Nations General Assembly resolution 3379, categorizing Zionism as a form of racism and racial discrimination. The only bright spot was the failure to achieve an African consensus as five countries—Côte d'Ivoire, Liberia, Malawi, Swaziland, and the Central African Republic—voted against the draft and sixteen other African countries abstained.

---

35 Oded, "Fifty Years of MASHAV Activity."

36 Shoshanna Solomon, "From 1950s Rationing to Modern High-Tech Boom: Israel's Economic Success Story," *Times of Israel*, April 18, 2018, https://www.timesofisrael.com/from-1950s-rationing-to-21st-century-high-tech-boom-an-economic-success-story/.

In the two years following the Yom Kippur War, Israel slashed 50 percent of MASHAV's operational budget.[37] The drastic budgetary cut didn't actually lead to a 50 percent reduction in activities.[38] Israel continued to send farmers, doctors, teachers, and other experts to provide assistance, including in countries that had cut off diplomatic relations, but did so under the auspices of the UN and other nongovernmental organizations (NGOs).[39] It cut funding for bilateral cooperation projects but continued to accept African trainees at its MASHAV facilities if they were funded by other multilateral institutions or by the beneficiaries themselves. The ongoing activity reinforced Foreign Minister Abba Eban's assertion that "the aid provided by MASHAV is not a tool for political activity but should be considered in its human context. We will try to respond positively to every request we receive even if our resources are very modest.... We will be happy if our cooperation leads to the creation of an atmosphere of friendship, because our activities are motivated by considerations of human brotherhood."[40]

Reflecting on this dark period, Golda said, "No one regrets more bitterly than I that, for the time being, certain African nations have chosen to turn their backs on us. But what really matters is what we—and they—accomplished together, what the thousands of Israeli experts in agriculture, hydrology, regional planning, public health, engineering, community services, medicine and scores of other fields actually did throughout Africa between 1958 and 1973, and what the thousands of Africans who trained in Israel during those years took home

---

37 Inbal and Zahavi, "The Rise and Fall of Israel's Bilateral Aid Budget," 14.

38 Inbal and Zahavi, "The Rise and Fall of Israel's Bilateral Aid Budget," 42.

39 Oded, "Fifty Years of MASHAV Activity."

40 Eban's circular to Israel's embassies, September 26, 1973, ISA 6737/25 [Hebrew].

with them. Those benefits can never be lost, and those achievements should never be minimized."[41]

Following the near-total collapse of relations with Africa in the early 1970s, the focus of Israel's aid program shifted to Latin America, which had continued to support Israel in multilateral forums. From 1974 until the early 1990s, more than two-thirds of the trainees in Israel came from Latin American counties.[42] In time, fractured relationships on the African continent were slowly rebuilt. Following the 1978 Camp David Accords, which paved the way for peace between Israel and Egypt, there was no longer a need for African nations to stand in solidarity with their "sister." Throughout the 1980s, Israel maintained relations with most of Latin America (except for Marxist Cuba, Guyana, and Nicaragua) and began making meaningful inroads into Asia. Aiding Israel's effort was the transformation of the global energy market. The growth of alternative energy and decline in global oil dependency weakened the influence of Arab nations that had used the Organization of the Petroleum Exporting Countries (OPEC) to sway international affairs by threatening an oil embargo.

The collapse of the Soviet Bloc in the early 1990s was another pivotal moment. An early supporter of the Zionist cause, the USSR voted in favor of the 1947 United Nations Partition Plan and recognized Israel three days after its establishment. When Israel emerged as a Western ally, the Soviets shifted their stance and backed the Arab regimes from the mid-1950s onward. The fall of the Soviet Union disrupted old loyalties and provided an inroad for Israel to improve its standing in both Africa and Asia. Throughout the 1990s, eighteen African

---

41 Meir, *My Life*, 307.

42 Inbal and Zahavi, "The Rise and Fall of Israel's Bilateral Aid Budget," 43.

countries renewed their ties and another eleven established relations for the first time. By 2023, Israel had diplomatic relations with all but six sub-Saharan African countries (Comoros, Somalia, Djibouti, Sudan, Niger, and Mali).

The major transformation in Israel's standing in Asia came about with the establishment of relations with Communist China in 1992. This in turn prompted a breakthrough in relations with India. A domino effect ensued as Israel soon forged diplomatic relations with Mongolia and Vietnam, and restored ties with Cambodia, Laos, South Korea, and Sri Lanka. It also established ties with fourteen Pacific states. Often these diplomatic relations went hand in hand with cooperation in the fields of security, agriculture, medicine, culture, science, and aviation.

Relations with the third Asian power, Japan, began to warm in the 1990s. Following the 1973 Yom Kippur War, Japan, resource-poor and heavily reliant on oil imports from Arab nations, had opted for economic pragmatism and condemned Israel. Following the collapse of the Arab economic boycott, ties between Tokyo and Jerusalem became increasingly open and cordial. In 1994, the two countries signed a culture and education agreement and the following year a science and technology cooperation agreement.

Since its founding, MASHAV has worked in 140 countries and trained hundreds of thousands of professionals all over the world, including from countries that still have no diplomatic relations with Israel. Working in five languages, MASHAV runs over a hundred courses in Israel and abroad each year that train in nine specialties: food security, education, public health, research and development, empowering civil society, promoting entrepreneurship, women's empowerment, rural and urban development, and humanitarian aid.

Currently, the development budget benchmark for member states is set at 0.7 percent of GNP. According to OECD data, in 2022 Israel allocated only around 0.1 percent of its gross national income (roughly $569 million USD) as Official Development Assistance (ODA).[43] That is one of the lowest of all developed countries worldwide. Since Israel's foreign aid budget encompasses bilateral and multilateral aid funds (such as payments to international organizations), MASHAV's annual spending is just over NIS 30 million ($8.5 million).[44]

International development long ceased to be a major focus of Israeli governments. One public opinion poll conducted in 2008 found that only 56 percent of Israelis believed Israel should aid developing countries at all, with a further 17 percent saying they were unsure.[45] MASHAV, once the largest department in Israel's Foreign Ministry, now operates on a shoestring budget. Retired MASHAV medical affairs advisor Dr. Yossi Baratz said in 2016, "With $10 million a year it is very difficult to routinely operate on the ground in 130 countries, and also designate funds for emergencies. Therefore, we build the solution according to our capabilities, and not according to the needs on the ground."[46]

---

[43] "Israel," in *Development Co-operation Profiles* (Paris: OECD Publishing, 2023), https://doi.org/10.1787/46d66229-en (accessed on July 30, 2023).

[44] Lee Landman, "Left Behind: Who Will Rescue the Israeli Foreign Aid Agency?," *The Arena* (Reichman University, Abba Eban Institute), May 2018.

[45] Aliza Inbal and Ophelie Namiech, "Israel70: A Light unto the Nations Once More? The Renaissance in Israel's International Development Assistance Programme," *Fathom*, July 2018, https://fathomjournal.org/israel70-a-light-unto-the-nations-once-more-the-renaissance-in-israels-international-development-assistance-programme/.

[46] Inbal and Namiech, "Israel70: A Light unto the Nations Once More?"

CHUTZPAH(ISM), IDEALISM, PRAGMATISM, AND ADVENTURISM

"For Israel, it is both a moral and a political issue and there is no doubt that Israel must look upon such aid as a historic mission, as necessary for Israel as it is beneficial to those we help."

—David Ben-Gurion

In the years leading to Israel's founding, the Jewish people fought to win security, sovereignty, and self-determination. The birth of their state gave rise to a new type of Jew—one who was self-sufficient and proudly independent. This new Jew would take the lessons of Jewish history and the aspirations born from Jewish values to contribute to the overall global condition.

For decades, MASHAV was the face of Israel's international development projects around the world. As its budget declined, Israeli citizens stepped forward to fill the void. By the 1990s, the field of international development and disaster relief began to take shape in Israel. During that decade, Israel's population grew by 35 percent, mainly owing to a large wave of immigration following the collapse of the Soviet Union. The new immigrants brought with them valuable scientific and professional expertise that fed the country's economy. This influx, coupled with the opening of new markets at the end of the Cold War and the onset of the Oslo Accords, energized Israel's economy. Israel enjoyed a remarkable economic expansion that brought new levels of prosperity and a significant increase in purchasing power.

Newfound prosperity combined with an optimism for peace contributed to the explosion of independent nonprofit organizations providing assistance outside Israel's borders. According to the Israel chapter of the Society for International Development (SID), there were just eight Israeli international development nonprofits before the year 2000. Twenty-five years later, SID counted under its umbrella eighty nonprofits and one thousand entities in the Israeli ecosystem, including civil society organizations, companies, government institutions, and academic forums acting in the fields of international development and humanitarian aid. The field is on a growth trajectory with a new generation of international development and humanitarian workers emerging to harness Israeli expertise and innovation in the service of international development.

Who are the pioneering Israelis behind these NGOs, and what compels them to leave the security of home to assist people all over the world? Why do so many women and men from low-income countries turn to Israel to acquire the knowledge and techniques to interrupt the cycle of poverty? Each story is unique, but four clear themes emerge: idealism, pragmatism, adventurism, and chutzpah(ism).

The idealists are inspired by the Jewish principle of *tikkun olam* (Hebrew for "repair the world"). They strive to be global citizens who contribute to the betterment of the overall global condition and feel a pressing moral obligation for Israel to contribute, as an expression of the Jewish ideal to do good in the world. Driven by that desire, they harness Israeli expertise together with cutting-edge innovation to address long-term sustainable development.

The pragmatists understand that Israel's innovative technologies, knowledge, and expertise can fundamentally transform the well-being of entire communities. They also sense opportunity and believe the growing markets of the future are in low-income countries.

The adventurists are fueled by adrenaline and a spirit of exploration. Eager to shake off the familiar, they travel far from home to immerse themselves in new cultures and communities. Along the way, they encounter great need and harness their spirit of entrepreneurship and discovery in service of others.

There is one more utterly audacious group of people who knowingly assume enormous personal risk by going behind enemy lines to assist desperate civilians in war zones. This group understands that as Israelis, if they are captured, they will likely face torture and certain death. These men and women are distinct in their courage and embodiment of chutzpah (Hebrew for "audacity").

Most of the individuals profiled in the chapters that follow embody a combination of idealism, pragmatism, adventurism, and chutzpah(ism). Each has a remarkable personal story and, when taken together, reflect the grit, determination, kindness, compassion, and heroism of Israel's international development field. They have proven that Israel isn't just a "Start-Up Nation"; it is also the Stand-Up Nation.

CHUTZPAH(ISM)

"The State of Israel will be tested not by its wealth, not by its army and not by its technique, but rather in its moral identity and humanitarian values."

—David Ben-Gurion

No democracy has faced the unrelenting series of threats that Israel has endured. It has been existentially challenged since the day it declared independence and has been forced to navigate war, terrorism, diplomatic isolation, and economic boycott while absorbing waves of anguished refugees. Israel has faltered but never failed. This success is often attributed to a uniquely Israeli quality—chutzpah—Hebrew for a blend of temerity, audacity, and gall. The combination has been a defining quality of Israel since its founding. Israeli chutzpah reflects a deep-seated belief in what is possible, and it manifests as a willingness to take risks, challenge the status quo, and push boundaries. Chutzpah is what it takes to set aside logic and put oneself in harm's way to save the lives of strangers, particularly when the consequences could be grave.

In 1949, a seventeen-year-old named Eliyahu Saranga left Istanbul to start a new life in Israel. His older brother, Shimon, also a passionate Zionist, had arrived in the newly founded state some months earlier and was serving in the IDF. With no way of knowing exactly when Eliyahu would come, Shimon walked to the port each day to search for his little brother. Lo and behold, one day he arrived to find Eliyahu standing with a single suitcase, inside of which was his one good outfit, a wool suit that had little use in his new sun-soaked country. Eliyahu joined Kibbutz Halutza in the south and began learning Hebrew but soon felt that he was better suited to living in a city and joined the Israeli navy.

That is how Eliyahu found himself a part of Israel's first international rescue mission, which was entirely unplanned. In 1953, the young country was building its navy and sent a small number of repurposed warships to conduct training exercises in the Aegean Sea. On August 12, as the Israeli ships were set to return home, SOS calls sounded off the Greek shores. A series of deadly earthquakes had struck the southern Ionian Islands. The event measured 7.3 on the Richter scale, raised the whole island of Kefalonia by sixty centimeters, and caused widespread damage.

The SOS signals were received simultaneously by three different fleets—the American Sixth Fleet, a group of British destroyers, and the Israeli navy. The commander of the tiny Israeli flotilla sent a preliminary report to naval headquarters in Haifa and requested permission to offer aid.

Israel of the 1950s was small, poor, and diplomatically isolated. A number of European countries had not yet recognized Israel, among them Germany, Austria, Ireland, Portugal, Spain, and Greece. For years, Greek public opinion was staunchly pro-Arab. There was no way to know how they would feel when they came face-to-face with Israeli sailors. Nonetheless, it didn't take long for the flotilla commander to receive a response from

Mordechai (Mocha) Limon, commander of the navy: "Enter and provide assistance."

The Israeli fleet sailed past the American and British fleets, which, because of the sheer size of their ships, could not access the areas of the islands that had been devastated. The arriving Israeli sailors saw huge blocks of land had fallen into the sea. Wide cracks and smoking fissures were visible throughout the island. Fires had broken out in the city, and streets lay in ruins.

As Eliyahu related to his son years later, the law of the sea at the time directed that the first rescue force to arrive on the scene takes command of the operation; and thus the fledgling nation that Greece snubbed assumed responsibility for directing rescue operations. Israeli sailors set up a relief center on the coast in Kefalonia to treat and evacuate thousands of Greeks to the mainland. Eliyahu was serving on a ship named *Achi Mivtach*. The ship's doctor helped a Greek woman deliver her baby, and she repaid his kindness by naming her newborn son "Mivtachos."[47] For three days, Eliyahu and the other Israeli sailors took supplies from their own ships to distribute food, water, and medicine to the injured. Other fleets began to arrive slowly and, with them, additional supplies.

When the operation ended, the king of Greece personally awarded badges of merit to the commanders of the operation and conveyed his sincere and deepest gratitude to Prime Minister David Ben-Gurion for providing help to the inhabitants of the island. The Greek press wrote dozens of articles and nicknamed the Israeli navy "the fleet of love and hope," and "the Israeli sailors of salvation."

---

[47] Itamar Eichner, "The Navy's Lost Greek Boy," Yedioth Archives, August 25, 2013.

Despite the outpouring of gratitude, it would take thirty-seven years for Greece to grant full diplomatic recognition to Israel. Early on, Israel learned that its efforts abroad didn't necessarily translate into political or diplomatic wins. Nonetheless, those sailors paved the way for future IDF humanitarian aid missions. Between 1953 and 2022, the Israel Defense Forces dispatched thirty-nine humanitarian aid missions all over the world, including inside the borders of enemy states.

In February 2023, a massive earthquake occurred in southern Turkey near the northern border of Syria. It was the most devastating one to hit earthquake-prone Turkey in over twenty years. More than fifteen thousand people were killed and tens of thousands injured. Freezing weather conditions complicated rescue efforts and further endangered survivors, as more than one hundred aftershocks struck the region.

Israel quickly mobilized a humanitarian relief team of IDF doctors, nurses, and search-and-rescue personnel. Joining the team was Eliyahu's son, David Saranga, who today serves as the head of Digital Diplomacy in Israel's Ministry of Foreign Affairs. The Israeli team landed in Adana in southern Turkey and slowly made their way to Kahramanmaraş, where the Turkish government had assigned them to operate. The area had been plunged into darkness when the earthquake knocked out electricity, and the only warmth and only light at night came from building fires.

The first of many international relief teams to arrive, the Israeli team got to work, speaking to survivors to find out where their family members may have been trapped and excavating through huge piles of rubble. David worked around the clock, coordinating with local authorities, as Israelis flew over planes of essential goods, food, and field hospitals to assist recovery efforts. For David, the experience held special meaning. "I always imagined going to visit Istanbul to see the neighborhood where my father was born and grew up." He continued: "Instead, my first time traveling to Turkey was because of the earthquakes. I kept thinking of my late father and how he ended up on a mission because of an earthquake. Now here I was all these years later helping the people of Turkey, a country my father loved and cherished very much."

"Because I was blessed by God."

—Eyal Dror

Operation Good Neighbor

Syria has remained technically at war with Israel since the Jewish state's founding in 1948. Anti-Israel rhetoric has been a long-standing feature of official Syrian discourse, and media outlets depict Israel, its people, and Jews overall as inherently untrustworthy and evil. Fear of being branded a collaborator or traitor kept Syrians from making contact with their Israeli neighbors for decades. This refusal to engage shifted when the Syrian civil war gave the Syrian people a greater enemy to fear.

The roots of the civil war began with the Arab Spring. In December 2010, a young Tunisian fruit vendor named Mohamed Bouazizi stood in front of the local municipal building, poured paint thinner over his body, and lit himself aflame. It was an act of protest against the rampant corruption and humiliation that had become a grating daily insult for the Tunisian people. Bouazizi's act sparked protests across Tunisia, which spread across the Middle East and North Africa, eventually forcing regime changes in Tunisia, Egypt, and Yemen. Inspired by these previously unthinkable events, a group of schoolchildren in the southwestern Syrian city of Deraa spray-painted on a school wall: "The people want the fall of the regime." The boys were arrested and tortured by the Syrian regime. Outraged demonstrators clashed with police, and protests spread. Syrians rallied for the release of political prisoners, greater freedoms, and an end to corruption.

Fearful of what he had witnessed in nearby Arab countries, Syrian President Bashar al-Assad's response was swift and brutal. The Syrian army fired on unarmed protesters and carried out mass arrests that indiscriminately swept up both dissidents and bystanders. Still, the protest continued. In 2011, the Syrian army laid siege to Deraa, cutting off access to food, water, medicine, and electricity. Across the country, Assad imposed sieges, conducted aerial bombardments, and even unleashed chemical weapons.

Al-Qaeda militants saw opportunity in the chaos. By early 2012, Jabhat al-Nusra announced itself as al-Qaeda's Syrian franchise. Soon after, a group that called itself the Islamic State of Iraq emerged and employed even more brutal tactics. Within months, jihadi groups established control over territory spanning eastern Syria and western Iraq. Syria descended into chaos, with hundreds of thousands of Syrians killed and millions displaced.[48]

Israel watched events unfold on its northern border with concern. While Syria was technically an enemy state, relative calm had prevailed on the border for forty years. The Assad regime kept the frontier quiet, while United Nations

[48] Zachary Laub, "Syria's Civil War: The Descent into Horror," Council on Foreign Relations, February 14, 2023, https://www.cfr.org/article/syrias-civil-war.

peacekeepers verified the limited deployments of Israeli and Syrian forces across a demilitarized ceasefire line. With the Syrian army driven from the area, Israel found itself uncomfortably close to a branch of the Islamic State, al-Qaeda-affiliated militants, and countless other armed jihadi groups committed to Israel's demise. The IDF also worried that Iranian and Lebanese Hezbollah operatives would use the cover of chaos to encroach and launch attacks. The war raging in Syria was easily seen and heard from the Israeli side of the border fence.

During routine patrols, IDF soldiers would sometimes see injured Syrians across the fence and throw over first aid kits or simple supplies they had on hand. As the war dragged on, military reports detailed the worsening humanitarian situation. Critical infrastructure had been destroyed, leaving huge swaths of the population without access to electricity or medical clinics. The IDF estimated that 70 percent of Syria's doctors had either fled or been killed in the fighting.

One winter night in February 2013, seven injured Syrians dragged themselves to the border fence and pleaded for help from a passing IDF patrol. A commander made the on-the-spot decision to provide care and save their lives. Word spread of the incident, and soon more injured Syrians arrived at the border, desperate for medical help. Some were men wounded in war; others were teenagers from a car accident, a boy bitten by a snake, and a woman who had a complication in childbirth. The casualties seemed endless. With Syria in tatters, more and more Syrians weighed the barbarism inside their country against the fear of being branded a Zionist collaborator and made the desperate choice to seek help from Israel.

With so many Syrians arriving at the border, Israel needed a plan. Discussions took place at the highest levels of military and government. The decision was made that Israel would not turn away people who desperately needed help. Some hoped that providing aid to Syrian refugees would allow Syrians to see Israelis as people rather than as a caricature of evil. And perhaps that would eventually create a more peaceful border.

With the decision made, the IDF needed someone to oversee the complex and secret operation, dubbed Operation Good Neighbor. They selected Eyal Dror. Eyal enlisted in the IDF shortly after the signing of the 1993 Oslo Accords, which led to the creation of a Palestinian Authority to assume governing responsibilities in the West Bank and Gaza Strip. The Coordination of Government Activities in the Territories, or COGAT, was set up by Israel to liaise with the Palestinian Authority. For two decades, Eyal served as an officer in COGAT working on security and civil coordination projects. He hadn't planned to spend a career in the military; but like his father, who retired as a major in the IDF, Eyal loved serving his country and each time his service term was about to end, he reenlisted for two more years. Those two-year stints eventually added up to twenty-four years, and Eyal rose to the rank of lieutenant colonel. Two decades working with Palestinians had made him fluent in Arabic, familiar with Arab culture, and adept at navigating the workings of NGOs and government offices. It was a skill set that was suited to the management of Operation Good Neighbor.

In June 2016, Eyal got a call from his commander, who explained the situation simply: "This is a national project and we need you." The mission directive was straightforward. Provide aid to thousands of desperate Syrians in the short term and stabilize the border in the long term by showing the neighboring population that Israel was not the enemy. Getting the mission up and running was anything but straightforward.

"I needed Waze to find my new base," Eyal relates with a laugh. "I had been in the army more than twenty years, but this was entirely new to me."

On his first day in command, he was handed a key and pointed in the direction of his office, which turned out to be an empty room. There were no computers or staff, so Eyal built the operation from the ground up. He interviewed soldiers and officers, set up a workspace, mapped the landscape of NGOs that could potentially assist with the efforts, and looked for ways to build communications channels inside Syria. Within a few months, Eyal's unit was ready to send food staples across the border, but they hadn't anticipated how the goods would be received.

"That first operation was a total failure," Eyal recalls. "We transferred food into Syria, and they burned it. A *fatwah*, a ruling issued by an Islamic court, had been circulated. It said that Syrians could receive lifesaving medical treatment from Israel, but anything beyond that was considered collaboration with the enemy."

Decades of suspicion and hate couldn't be undone overnight. Eyal narrowed his focus to delivering medical supplies while learning more about the beliefs and habits of the people he was trying to help. He hoped to partner with large humanitarian aid organizations on the ground in Syria; but when he approached them many outright refused, while others felt their dollars would be better spent in Aleppo or elsewhere. They were afraid that if the regime found out they were partnering with Israel, they would endanger the lives of their staff. Eyal was patient and persistent. He explored every avenue he could find to send medicine and medical equipment across the border. One partner was an Israeli NGO called Israeli Flying Aid. Together they raised 1.4 million shekels (a little over $400,000 USD) to buy tons of medicine. In time, he also secured a partnership with Rahma Relief, a Muslim NGO, which donated 300 million shekels' ($87 million USD) worth of equipment and medicine to Syrian clinics.

Another agreement was forged with a Louisiana-based Christian humanitarian organization called Friend Ships Unlimited, which had opened a medical clinic called Mazor Ladach (Hebrew for "assistance to the unfortunate") in territory that, while still legally Israel, was nearly as dangerous as being in Syria. The medical camp consisted of several enormous tents joined together in a tight circle. Staffed by devout Christian Americans, the team slept in the camp and returned to Israel with an IDF escort twice a week. Around three hundred Syrians could receive medical care every week without the fear of crossing into Israel and being tarred as a collaborator. "I don't know how many times in history a Christian and a Muslim and a Jewish organization cooperated to help Muslims. And did so under the command of an Israeli officer," Eyal says with a chuckle.

When he was appointed to head Operation Good Neighbor, Eyal's orders were to provide humanitarian aid to the population within one to two kilometers of the Israeli border. The more ways he found to help, the further Israel's support extended, eventually stretching as far as forty kilometers inside Syria. Eyal found the funds to build a maternity hospital in a Syrian village and navigated complex channels to get medical treatment for Syrian children with chronic illnesses.

A father himself, Eyal was moved by the Syrian children he met. "I would see young kids who'd been brought to Israel for treatment fall down and get hurt, but not cry," Eyal began. "I couldn't understand it until a Syrian mother explained that the children didn't cry because they'd learned long ago in Syria that nobody would come to help them even if they did cry."

One of his prized possessions is a picture from a nine-year-old Syrian girl. She arrived at the border fence suffering from diabetes. IDF medics assessed the urgency of her situation, and she was transported to an Israeli hospital for lifesaving treatment. "When she was well enough to go home," Eyal recounts, "she drew me a picture as a present. She drew an Israeli flag, added her name in Arabic, then a heart, then my name in Arabic." Another memory that stands out for Eyal is playing soccer with a Syrian boy. He ran after the child chasing the ball and, stopping to catch his breath, asked the boy, "Aren't you afraid of me?" The boy laughed and answered, "You're an Israeli officer not a Syrian soldier. Why should I be afraid?"

On any given night, the IDF was active on multiple points on the Syrian frontier, interacting with locals to transfer goods and assessing serious medical cases. When treatment in a field hospital wasn't possible, the IDF coordinated evacuations to Israeli hospitals. Israel's medical facilities are a microcosm of society and a place where Jews, Muslims, Christians, Druze, and others work alongside one another every day. Injured Syrians were shocked to discover Israeli doctors, nurses, and paramedics who spoke Arabic and prayed to Allah. And they couldn't believe that the Jews treated their Arab colleagues with respect.

The IDF knew that terror groups could easily take advantage of the humanitarian work to launch an attack. The topography of the region was such that the enemy was on higher terrain and had a strategic advantage. Every night brought with it the worry of an ambush, sniper, missile launch, or IED, but still Operation Good Neighbor continued. The IDF's policy was not to check IDs to see if the injured were rebel fighters. After a pat-down at the border, anyone in need of aid was given medical care. It was an enormous risk. When Syrians returned to Syria, they lied about where they'd been. Medications with Hebrew writing had the labels removed to ensure there was no evidence of where they had been.

Eyal's efforts to build trust paid off. His Syrian partners affectionately called him "Abu Yakub," which is Arabic for Father of Yakub. (Eyal's father, Yaakov—which is the Hebrew form of the Arabic name Yakub—had passed away shortly before Eyal began his work with Syria, and Eyal honored his memory by taking his name.)

A year after Operation Good Neighbor began, the *fatwah* on Israeli support was lifted, and the IDF was able to transfer hundreds of thousands of tons of food, baby formula, medicine, clothes, fuel, generators, and piping for water wells into Syria. Over 400 million shekels ($116 million USD) in donations of food, clothes, and other lifesaving necessities were transported into Syria.

Around the same time, discussions took place within the IDF to make the operation public. Eyal was reluctant. He worried that the goodwill he had built up would be destroyed if his Syrian partners felt they were being used as PR tools. He asked his contacts in Syria for their opinion and was surprised when they told him to tell the world. They asked him to be their voice since it seemed the world was blind and deaf to their pain. Shortly afterward, Israel's work in Syria made international headlines.

By June 2018, Operation Good Neighbor was winding down. The Syrian army was advancing north and quickly regaining territory. Once they reached the border, Assad wouldn't tolerate ongoing Israeli assistance and would forcefully reimpose the message to Syrians that Israel was a sworn enemy.

Eyal was driving home late one evening when his commander called to say that there was an emerging and urgent situation with the White Helmets. Officially known as the Syrian Civil Defense, the White Helmets—nicknamed for their signature protective hats—were Syrian rescue workers who dug people out of the rubble following government airstrikes. Before the war, these individuals were teachers, bakers, engineers, pharmacists, carpenters, and students. During the war, their bravery saved more than one hundred thousand Syrian lives.[49] The Syrian government had accused the group of being traitors who conspired with terrorists to demonize Assad.

As the Syrian army recaptured territory, men and women of the White Helmets fled with their families to the Israeli border. As their fate grew increasingly precarious, Western governments requested assistance from Israel and Jordan. Early on a Friday morning, Eyal received instructions to return to the base. The army needed someone with contacts inside Syria who had enough trust to be able to locate, assemble, and move the White Helmets to an extraction point. Eyal had developed close relationships with Syrian village elders and heads of local councils, and their help would be critical to save the lives of the White Helmets in a high-risk, top-secret mission.

---

[49] Foreign Secretary Jeremy Hunt and International Development Secretary Penny Mordaunt, United Kingdom Foreign & Commonwealth Office, Department for International Development, "Resettlement of White Helmets from Syria: Statement," press release, July 22, 2018, https://www.gov.uk/government/news/statement-on-white-helmets.

On Saturday night, the IDF picked up about a hundred White Helmets and some three hundred of their family members. "We opened the gate between Israel and Syria, a potential flash point for attacks, for ten hours," Eyal says. "That was a huge amount of time given the ferociousness of the fighting. White Helmet volunteers and their families poured through the border," he continues. "Four hundred and twenty-two people crossed into Israel that night, including babies and children." They were ferried in buses across the Golan Heights to Jordan, where they stayed until they could be permanently resettled in Europe.

By the time Operation Good Neighbor came to an end in 2018, Eyal's unit had overseen seven hundred humanitarian operations. Their efforts had seen eight thousand Syrians treated in field clinics, fourteen hundred Syrian children treated for chronic diseases, one thousand babies born in the maternity hospital, and forty-five hundred Syrians receive lifesaving treatment paid for by Israel inside of Israel.

Eyal retired from the IDF making Operation Good Neighbor the highlight of his career. Thinking back on why he was chosen out of everyone to lead this mission, he says, "Because I was blessed by God."

"My boss is my conscience."

—Gal Lusky

Israeli Flying Aid

A critical partner in the success of Operation Good Neighbor was Israeli Flying Aid (IFA), Israel's most audacious and daring nonprofit. Gal Lusky and her teams of volunteers enter countries that don't have diplomatic relations with Israel or refuse humanitarian aid to bring lifesaving relief to vulnerable people.

"Sometimes people will say to me: 'Who is your boss?'" Gal shares. "They think maybe it's the Israeli government or the Mossad. But that's not it. My boss is my conscience."

Gal and her team were in Darfur distributing lifesaving assistance during the genocide. They were in Indonesia following a devastating string of earthquakes and in Burma after a cyclone destroyed critical infrastructure. When floods destroyed villages in northeastern Georgia near the border with Chechnya in 2005, the Georgian government claimed it was too dangerous to send aid. IFA found their way in and delivered tons of food. IFA has sent volunteers into the Kashmir region, on both sides of the border, in India and Pakistan.

Each of IFA's missions is dangerous and complex. In many ways, Gal's childhood prepared her for this work. Born in 1968, she and her younger brother, Yaron, grew up on Kibbutz Hukok on the shores of the Sea of Galilee. They lived alongside all the kibbutz's children in a designated house with a caregiver. Gal was the only girl living with eight boys from just three weeks of age until she turned eighteen. Children's houses on kibbutzim have fallen out of favor, but Gal believes her childhood instilled in her independence and a sense of responsibility for others. So much so that she once gave her mother's washing machine to a needy, single immigrant mother in a nearby town without first getting her own mother's permission. She figured her mother could get by with the kibbutz laundry facilities.

After high school, Gal learned that the kibbutz could only afford to pay university tuition for two young people each year. Gal added her name to the list of prospective students but recognized that it would be years before it would be her turn. Instead, she moved, penniless, to Tel Aviv and found part-time jobs—first as a flight attendant for the domestic airline Arkia and later selling bumper stickers—to pay for her criminology degree. Saving fastidiously, she covered tuition and even scraped together the money for a down payment on an apartment. By the time she was twenty-four, Gal thought she had things figured out.

Everything changed when her brother, Yaron, was injured in battle. While serving as a paratrooper commander in southern Lebanon, Yaron was shot by Hezbollah forces. He was evacuated by helicopter with serious injuries to his head, eyes, and hand. The doctors said his condition was critical. Gal rushed to the hospital and remained at her brother's side through months of surgeries and the long convalescence at home. Yaron eventually recovered and returned to military service, but by then Gal's outlook and priorities had changed dramatically and she couldn't envision returning to her old life. Gal explains, "After my brother was wounded, I felt that I had two options: spend my life seeking revenge against those who hurt him or learn compassion and do something with the privilege of being born in a strong and developed country with medical infrastructure unmatched in the Middle East. I decided I would be there for people who are much less fortunate than me."

It was 1994 and television screens were filled with horrific images from the aftermath of the genocide against the Tutsi in Rwanda. Gal felt a pull to help. She had never been to an African country, didn't know anyone on the continent, and had no experience in the world of international development. She bought a one-way ticket and took off with just $5000 in her pocket. Once in Rwanda, she joined an NGO working to reunite families torn apart by the civil war. The desire to help became addictive, and Gal spent the next decade bouncing between disasters, both natural and man-made, trying to help the people who needed it most.

In late 2004, a 9.1-magnitude earthquake ripped through an undersea fault in the Indian Ocean, propelling a massive column of water toward unsuspecting shores. That tsunami would be the deadliest in recorded history, wiping out a staggering 230,000 lives in a matter of hours. Gal led an Israeli team of volunteers to save lives in Sri Lanka. That mission proved to be a turning point. For years, she had watched in frustration when humanitarian aid didn't reach the most desperate and needy groups. The reason was often ugly politics. Assistance can only be brought into a country with the approval of the local government or ruling regime. Without explicit permission, NGOs won't enter a region even if it's devasted by natural disaster, war, or genocide. In Sri Lanka, the government had allowed aid agencies to enter the country but used the cover of chaos to establish no-go zones to block aid from reaching the Tamil Tigers, an ethnic minority fighting to establish an independent Tamil state. The Tamils were living in the region hardest hit by the tsunami.

Politics didn't interest Gal. She was appalled to see aid being withheld as a tool of warfare. "The Sri Lankan government used that disaster to starve people," Gal explains. "They didn't let any organization help or send aid. All the major aid organizations knew the government was starving and preventing medical aid from reaching the Tamils and I couldn't live with this lie. If you prevent people from having access to clean water, medicine, or shelter, it's an act of murder. Simple as that. You may not be using weapons against them, but in my mind, blocking aid is a type of weapon."

Setting aside her own safety, Gal managed to enter the besieged Tamil area. "I snuck into the no-go zones and distributed forty-two thousand meals," she recounts. "That was the first time we brought Israeli volunteers like doctors and psychologists who specialize in treating children in post-trauma. It was our first operation."

Sri Lanka was just the beginning. For years, Gal had watched authoritarian governments declare areas as closed military zones or find some other excuse to prevent rescue crews from reaching victims. They would block any form of humanitarian aid from reaching groups branded enemies of the government.

"I came to see a horrific hypocrisy in Chapter VII of the United Nations Charter," Gal says with disgust. "The Charter sets out the Security Council's powers to maintain peace and identify threats and then take action to restore international peace and security. The big loophole is humanitarian aid. Nobody thought to make the intentional prevention of aid illegal." Gal continues, "It took me a while to figure it out, but after a decade working in disaster zones, I saw the dark side of humanitarian aid. Governments use catastrophe as a weapon against children and women whose only sin was to be born on the wrong side of the political map in their country.

"The UN and the humanitarian organizations know this, and everyone quietly goes along with it," Gal says with frustration. "In Pakistan, for example, why should the wives and children of the Kashmir rebels freeze to death in minus twelve-degree temperatures after an earthquake? Why should Tamil families in Sri Lanka be starved to death? These things happened and there was not a single condemnation by the UN Human Rights Council. The world is silent."

Gal refused to be silent. She founded Israeli Flying Aid (IFA) in 2005 on the premise that nobody asks permission to kill, so she won't ask permission to save lives. That sentiment became the organization's motto. IFA is unique in that it focuses on countries that have no diplomatic relations with Israel. That means that IFA operates in countries that are openly hostile to Israel and where the consequences would be particularly brutal if Israelis were discovered on the ground.

Volunteers make their way into target countries keeping their true identities below the radar. They do so to protect their own lives and minimize the risk to aid recipients who could be accused of being collaborators. Once the work is done, volunteers quietly leave, almost never making it known that they were ever there. Technically speaking, Gal is violating the law: Israeli law prohibits citizens from entering enemy countries. There is also a law that compels Israel to take significant action to bring home citizens who are kidnapped. Every IFA volunteer signs a waiver to release the Israeli government from that obligation. As Gal explains, "We're all adults. We don't want to hold our country responsible for a personal choice we knowingly made to save other lives." As an afterthought, she shares, "It's almost impossible for me to secure complete insurance coverage for my team."

Gal builds her teams around the needs of the crisis. "Following an earthquake, I need orthopedic and internal medicine doctors, and specialists in search-and-rescue," she says. "If it's a fire, I need medical professionals who are experts with burns and air passages." For the most dangerous and secretive missions, she calls on volunteers who served in elite units of the IDF. "Our great heroes are a group of Muslim, Christian, and Druze volunteers who retired from elite units in the IDF," Gal explains. "These guys have internalized that the real danger is not dying but living without the ability to do good in the world."

In some ways, they are taking the biggest risk. A Jew caught in Syria would be considered an enemy, and enemies have a value in that they can be exchanged for something. A Muslim caught in Syria would be viewed as a traitor, and that would be viewed with a particular hatred. Gal continues, "I send people I trust. They are the best in the world at what they do and know how to navigate difficult terrain and improvise when things go wrong. We could make a film out of every operation. There is always action, but no one does it for the action. We go to save lives. Period."

Over the years, Gal and her volunteers have been arrested, shot at, and suffered shrapnel wounds. The fear of what could go wrong, especially to her volunteers, never subsides.

"I'm scared every time," Gal admits. "It's difficult to maintain a cover story for an extended period. There's really no way to know if the team has been exposed. There's no way of making sure that one of the locals we work with won't betray us. There's no limit to the terrible things that could happen, but I can't concentrate on that."

When working in a country that is hostile to Israel, she tries to bring along the smallest possible team, and she insists on joining every mission. "I can't imagine putting anyone at risk without being right there with them." Many of the volunteers have post-traumatic stress disorder from their days in the IDF. That carries an additional operational risk because something may trigger them, but Gal won't turn them away. "A volunteer once asked me,

'I was taught to fight for the State of Israel and today I am not good enough to save a life?'"

Recipients of aid will most likely never know Israelis were involved. Gal isn't interested in credit. "Our goal isn't to change what people think about Israel. I don't care about anything except that their children will have something to eat or that the wounded will receive proper treatment. We go on missions to save lives. On our missions, there is no Star of David." Outside of danger zones, Gal is a proud and outspoken Zionist. "I decided to establish an organization registered in Israel that would be unapologetically Zionist. I hate it when Israelis apologize for our existence as a nation. Israel is not perfect, fine. But it's not by chance that I dedicate my life to saving lives. I do it because I am Jewish, Israeli, and Zionist, because of the education I received on the kibbutz. Jewish people sanctify life, and we need to take that mission to the world."

The Israeli government is obviously aware of IFA's work and has never interfered with a mission, even when the risk seemed unimaginably high. After twenty years of operations, Gal is plagued by the missions that went wrong.

"My biggest failure was in Haiti. We went there after the 2010 earthquake. We went into orphanages to give them medical help, and especially to make them happy. We decided to adopt an orphanage of seventy-five girls that collapsed completely and build them a new orphanage. The problem was we could not be there all the time to run all things, and some of our girls were sold for fifty dollars to be used as victims in voodoo ceremonies."

She continues, "I can't get it through my mind even to this day. Murder of innocent girls for worship, human sacrifice. Not only does this phenomenon still exist, but it has become an institutionalized ritual. It was a jarring failure. Afterward, I understood it was necessary to protect the girls, and for that we had to close the orphanage and move them to another place."

Gal has tried to take lessons from the tragedies. Today, IFA supports two orphanages, one in Chad that opened before Israel had diplomatic relations with the north-central African country. Gal won't say the location of the second orphanage, but she explains why IFA has taken on this responsibility, "Muslim orphans need more attention since their status in Islam is complex and sensitive. There is no legal adoption; therefore, orphans can't carry the family name of an adoptive family or be a part of that family's heritage. Worse, there are countries where orphans are taken as slaves or servants." IFA's orphanages are run by local staff, and Israeli volunteers visit a few times a year to provide extra support, help with construction projects, or purchase supplies. They make arrangements with the local hospitals to ensure the children can get treatment and medicine, and they have Israeli doctors review complicated cases.

Over the years, some of IFA's operations have surfaced in the public eye. The nonprofit became front-page news when the world learned that an Israeli group had spent years helping Syrians during the Syrian civil war. "It was happening on our border," Gal recounts. "The Assad regime committed unspeakable atrocities and crimes against humanity." Schools, hospitals, and homes were bombed daily. Chemical weapons, banned by international law, were used against civilians. The regime employed execution-style murders and mass rapes, silencing dissenters through death and torture.

Gal and her team got to work. "We called on Israelis to help. We worked with Israeli youth movements and other organizations to collect critical aid and tons of winter gear that we then transferred across the border to Syrians. Children were freezing to death in Syria," she continues, "and when children in Israeli youth movements heard that we wanted to collect items for these victims, they immediately started knocking on doors. Within two weeks they collected seventy tons of coats, blankets, and sleeping bags. These were all delivered a week later."

It was complicated and dangerous. Fearful for the safety of her volunteers working on the Israeli-Syrian border, where people were more likely to shoot than ask questions, they arranged to transfer supplies via two neighboring countries. They were so efficient and successful at transferring lifesaving goods across the border that, in 2016, the IDF invited them to join a pilot for a cross-border mission in which supplies were sent from Israel to the Syrian part of the Golan.

The media attention brought on by the Syrian civil war has long since died down. Away from the spotlight, IFA runs four or five operations simultaneously in locations around the world. For years, Gal led the entire operation on her own. Today, the organization is run by three women who call on a pool of twelve hundred volunteers.

"With more resources, there is so much more we could do," Gal says. "We need donors who do not request credit since most missions stay away from the public eye and media. Any time money comes in, we deploy a mission." And she'll continue to do so. "Over the years, I have realized that the only fear I have that is stronger than the fear of dying, is the fear of living my life without meaning." She adds, "I have chosen to have children, and it is my responsibility to leave the world to them a little better than how I received it."

"To be very honest, I had no idea how to take them out."

—Yotam Polizer

IsraAID in Afghanistan

In 2021, another Israeli nonprofit unexpectedly found itself directing lifesaving operations behind enemy lines.

On April 14, 2021, President Joe Biden, speaking from the White House, declared, "It's time to end the forever war." Within months, the last American military flight took off from Kabul International Airport, and the Taliban were once again in charge in Afghanistan. But the war wasn't over, not for the Afghan people. Tens of thousands of people feared oppression and reprisals by the Taliban—women and girls, ethnic and religious minorities, educators, judges who had imprisoned Taliban fighters, and the countless Afghans who had worked for the US government and military.

Organizations and individuals worked frenetically to devise rescue plans, including an Israeli organization called IsraAID.

"We're not a rescue organization," Yotam Polizer, IsraAID's global CEO, makes clear. "We are a nonpolitical, nongovernmental aid organization that responds to humanitarian crises and provides immediate relief and long-term recovery and resilience. We have worked in sixty-four countries and always with local partners on the ground."

IsraAID had never worked in an active war zone or attempted a rescue mission. And in Afghanistan, the stakes were high. The Taliban, after returning to power, declared that Israel was the only country with which its government would not form relations. As the situation grew increasingly dire, Yotam got desperate phone calls from people looking for a way to rescue friends and contacts in Afghanistan. With each call, Yotam had to explain that IsraAID didn't have a team in Afghanistan and had no way to help.

By the end of August, as the last American troops were preparing to depart, Yotam received three phone calls that sent IsraAID into uncharted territory. The first came from a couple of Israeli journalists who were in touch with members of the Afghani girls' robotics team and were desperately trying to escape the country. The next call came from a prominent philanthropist. He was looking for a way to rescue the Afghani female cycling team. A third call came from a friend named Sam (name changed to protect his identity), who claimed to have links to the Taliban and who offered to secure safe passage for people looking to flee the country.

It was a massive gamble. Yotam didn't know if Sam's contacts could be trusted. The evacuees would need to assume enormous personal risk. And IsraAID still had no direct contacts on the ground to intervene. The alternative, leaving the girls and women to the mercy of the Taliban, cinched the decision. IsraAID would attempt a daring rescue mission in Afghanistan.

A team was dispatched to quietly locate and collect the evacuees from across Kabul without alerting the Taliban. Some were already in hiding. The evacuees included members of the female cycling team and robotics team, a few of their relatives, and several human rights activists. They tried to evacuate the groups through Kabul's main international airport but were met with sheer chaos. Thousands of desperate Afghans swarmed the airport, mobbing the runways and clambering atop the wings of jets. Hundreds of people ran alongside an American military C-17 cargo plane, and some even tried to climb into the wheel wells or cling to the sides of the plane as it gathered speed. The world watched news coverage in horror as Afghans were either crushed by the plane on takeoff or fell to their deaths. Amidst the chaos, a suicide bomber detonated a vest packed with explosives and ball bearings. Thirteen US service members and an estimated 170 Afghans were killed in the blast.

It was clear that escaping via the airport wouldn't work. The rescue team pivoted to attempting a land evacuation through neighboring Tajikistan. Sam's contact in the Taliban organized a permit that would allow the evacuees to cross checkpoints on a bus chartered by IsraAID. Clad in burkas, forty-two young women and their families were able to pass through five Taliban checkpoints and arrived at the border. The next challenge was getting someone to convince Tajikistan to open its border. Yotam called longtime friend Carly Maisel, global CEO of Kirsh Philanthropies, and skipping the pleasantries, left an urgent message that said: "Carly, we need help evacuating people from Afghanistan and need someone who can get the Tajik border open." Carly admits, "I had to look up where Tajikistan was on a map." But once she realized what Yotam was attempting, she got to work, making hundreds of phone calls trying to find someone who could help. "It took three days and two very long nights to find a contact," Carly recalls.

Meanwhile the evacuees were at the border, surrounded by Taliban members who started asking them questions. "They would send us frantic messages," Yotam says. "So, we were able to keep in touch with them as these intense diplomatic efforts were under way." Most of the evacuees didn't know that a group of Israelis were working frantically to save their lives. "After three days," Yotam adds, "we understood that there was only one person who could approve opening the border and that was the president of Tajikistan. Once we knew it, we used every contact we had to reach him."

Carly continues, "He received five or six phone calls before finally acquiescing and giving the order to let the bus pass through the border." There was just one condition. Yotam had to personally guarantee that the refugees would stay in Tajikistan for no more than twenty-four hours. "To be very honest, I had no idea how to take them out," Yotam admits. "But given the circumstances, I agreed immediately."

The evacuees crossed safely into Tajikistan and were met by Israeli aid workers in the capital of Dushanbe. The team that had been working behind the scenes rejoiced. Joy quickly turned to anxiety as Yotam realized that he had one day to find the refugees a place to go. Carly and Yotam began another round of phone calls and eventually found an Emirati contact who was willing to call Sheikh Mohamed bin Zayed Al Nahyan (MBZ), then crown prince of Abu Dhabi.

Within thirty minutes, Yotam got a phone call saying that the UAE would take the refugees. It was a few months shy of the first anniversary of the Abraham Accords, and it would be the first joint humanitarian project between Israel and the UAE, a very real sign of the growing cooperation between the former enemy nations.

It took almost seventy-two hours to arrange transit visas to the UAE and a rescue flight. Things were falling into place when Yotam realized they had another enormous problem. Half of the refugees didn't have a passport, and without a passport they couldn't board the rescue flight. He called a good friend who traveled in diplomatic circles, and she reached out to the wife of a high-level Afghan diplomat who wasn't aligned with the Taliban. He agreed to issue the necessary passports. They were sent to Tajikistan via diplomatic courier and delivered to the waiting refugees. When they landed in the UAE, Yotam was there to greet them. The UAE set up a humanitarian city for refugees where they could access essential goods and get medical assistance, while IsraAID worked on arranging permanent resettlement in the United States and Canada.

Details of the harrowing mission were published in a British newspaper. It didn't take long before IsraAID was fielding hundreds of requests from other Afghans begging for help. There were more family members of the robotics team, as well as members of the women's cycling team, who hadn't been able to evacuate on the bus and were terrified of Taliban reprisals. Yotam got calls from the family members of Afghan diplomats, human rights activists, journalists, female judges who had prosecuted members of the Taliban, and a particularly desperate phone call from the family of the last Jewish woman in Afghanistan. Her Canadian daughter pleaded for Yotam to save her eighty-three-year-old mother.

"We figured we'd plan another, bigger operation. It was sheer chutzpah, and we were very naïve." Yotam went on. "We thought we would still have the permit from the Taliban, that our contact would prepare passports again, that the UAE would take more people. So, we decided to rescue one hundred people, and it didn't take long for that number to grow to one hundred and twenty-five, including four pregnant women and some babies."

IsraAID chartered three buses that would depart Kabul and follow the same route to evacuate through the Tajiki border. The buses were on track until they reached the last checkpoint, and the Taliban refused to allow passage. The frightened evacuees found a place to stay near the border while Yotam and his team tried to find a solution. As time passed, the messages from evacuees were increasingly panicked. The Taliban started collecting their names and separating out the men. It was beginning to look like a hostage situation. Try as he might, Yotam couldn't find a contact to navigate a request through the Taliban leadership, until he found someone in the Global Cyclist Association with a member in Qatar, a country that has diplomatic relations with the Taliban. The contact started making phone calls. Meanwhile, the evacuees were doing their best to negotiate their own way out of the situation. The Taliban had instructed them to return to their homes, adding that if they tried to cross the border again, they'd be killed. "I felt like we had to call off the operation," Yotam says. "We couldn't do something that would risk the lives of these people."

Another contact let IsraAID know that there were evacuation flights originating at Mazār-i-Sharīf on the northern border with Tajikistan. Desperate, they decided to send the group to that crossing, hoping they would find safe passage. Once again, they had to navigate the issue of securing passports. Of the 125 evacuees, 41 didn't have passports. They contacted the same Afghan diplomat, who issued new passports and sent them to a particularly remote part of the desert between Tajikistan and Afghanistan. The plan was to have a messenger on the Afghan side pick them up and bring them to the evacuees. It was another risky move, but Yotam didn't see any alternatives.

Word came through that the messenger had picked up the passports, but then IsraAID agents had to wait to hear if they reached the evacuees. Agonizing hours passed before they heard that the passports had been confiscated by the Taliban. Yotam called his Qatari contact in the cycling association and pleaded for intervention. Finally, word came back that if the owner of each passport would present him or herself to the Taliban, the passports would be handed over.

Tense consultations ensued between the IsraAID team and the evacuees. It was an enormous risk. The evacuees ultimately decided to take the chance, and one brave family member went to claim seven passports for members of his family. He returned with passports in hand. Over the course of the next twenty-four hours, each evacuee went until all the passports were claimed.

At long last, the group reached the airport, and following further harassment from the Taliban, they were able to board a flight and take off for Tajikistan. This time, the Tajiks were less receptive to the idea of opening their border and insisted that the refugees transit through their country as quickly as possible. It was proving harder to get approval from the UAE to send another group of refugees. It had been a month since the first mission. The UAE had absorbed large numbers of refugees and were now requiring incoming refugees to have a visa to their final resettlement location. Knowing it would take months to secure visas and knowing the Tajiks were unwilling hosts, a new plan had to be devised.

A few days earlier, Carly's boss, Wendy Fisher, had been in New York hosting an event for the Nizami Ganjavi International Center, an Azerbaijani think tank. In attendance were many current and former leaders from the Balkans, including Edi Rama, the prime minister of Albania. As it so happened, Albania had earned global accolades for its considerable efforts to take in refugees, a fact the prime minister proudly referenced in his speech that night. When Yotam called, frantic to find a safe haven for the second group of Afghans, Carly called Wendy. Hoping for a miracle, Wendy called Prime Minister Rama, whose words echoed in her mind. She explained the plight of the Afghan refugees, and he promised to investigate. A few minutes later, the foreign minister of Albania was on the line to say that if the Israeli team had a sound vetting process and the ability to transport the group, Albania would take them. Twelve hours later, 125 Afghan refugees landed in Albania.

One of the arriving refugees was Tova Moradi, the last living Jew in Afghanistan. Two of her children and four of her grandchildren were a part of IsraAID's second evacuation. Tova was one of ten children born to a Jewish family in Kabul. At the age of sixteen, she ran away from home and married a Muslim man. As she tells it, while the local Jewish community disavowed her, she never converted to Islam and maintained some Jewish traditions. Despite the friction over the marriage, Tova stayed in touch with family members over the years. Her parents and siblings fled Afghanistan, and some settled in Israel.

When the Taliban first seized power in Afghanistan in the 1990s, four of Tova's children left Afghanistan for Canada. Tova chose to stay and keep a low profile. She risked her life by hiding one of the few remaining Afghan Jews from the Taliban. Rabbi Isaak Levi arrived at her home one day, desperate to escape the Taliban. Tova's family planned to smuggle Isaak out of the country, but his health declined, and he passed away in 2005.

When the Taliban returned to power in 2021, Tova and her family feared for their lives. A daughter in Canada read about the IsraAID evacuation and reached out to the Israeli government for help, which in turn, reached out to IsraAID. From the safety of the town of Golem, where Afghan refugees were given shelter by the Albanian government, Tova video-called her sisters, some of whom she hadn't spoken to in half a century.

Thanks to IsraAID's efforts, 167 Afghan lives were saved. Only when they were finally safe did the evacuees learn that an

Israeli group was behind their rescue. One evacuee, a woman named Kawsar, recounts, "The moment they announced that the plane had landed was the happiest moment of my life. I cried tears of joy. At the border, I met Yotam, and I saw the IsraAID logo. I said to him, 'Hi, I know what aid is, but what's the rest of it?' He explained to me that it was an Israeli organization, and I just couldn't understand what or why. I was in shock, why were they helping Afghans? I couldn't understand; there was no connection between us."

Stunned and grateful, the Afghans couldn't believe that Israelis had come to their rescue. Their gratitude has not abated. "To this day," Yotam shares, "my team and I still get Shabbat Shalom messages every Friday. They are so very grateful."

Yotam's Postscript

Two days after the October 7 Hamas massacre in southern Israel, I received this note from former Afghan ambassador to the United States, Said Jawad:

Yotam, my friend.

I am writing with a very heavy heart to express my deepest condolences and profound sympathy for the recent barbaric terrorist attacks in Israel. I hope your family, friends and loved ones are safe.

The news of the terrorist attack is devastating, and my thoughts have been with you and my friends in Israel during this difficult time. I personally feel that pain and grief, as my own people have experienced the horrors of terrorism for decades. I understand all too well the profound impact such acts of violence can have on individuals, families, and communities.

The strength and resilience of the Jewish community show the power of human spirit in the face of savagery and callousness. Please know that we are here for you, as a friend and as someone who profoundly feels your pain.

May the memories of the innocent victims be a blessing, and may their families find solace in the support of friends during these very difficult times. My thoughts and prayers are with you, with families of the victims, and all those affected by this terrible tragedy.

With heartfelt sympathy and solidarity,
Ambassador Said Jawad

IDEALISM

"Israel has been granted a great, historic privilege, which is also a duty...helping to solve the central problems of all humanity."

—David Ben-Gurion

In the 1930s, a young Jewish engineer named Simcha Blass immigrated to British Mandate Palestine. Born into a Polish Hasidic family, Simcha had spent his youth with the local Zionist youth group. When World War I broke out, he was drafted into the Polish army and following his release studied engineering. He had always enjoyed tinkering with machines, and his passion for engineering was only overshadowed by his desire to help build a Jewish state.

In British-administered Palestine, he found that there wasn't much infrastructure, and so he applied his skills, eventually becoming one of Israel's leading water experts. He conceived and designed the plan that became the National Water Carrier and formed a close working relationship with Levi Eshkol, Israel's third prime minister, to form Mekorot, Israel's national water company.

One day in the early 1930s, while visiting a friend's home in Hadera, Simcha noticed a line of trees that caught his interest. One of the trees was much taller than the rest—even though they were all the same species, likely planted at the same time, and they all had the same soil, sun, and rainfall. Intrigued, he went to investigate and found that the three-quarter-inch metal pipe that brought water to the house had a small crack in it and was slowly leaking water, drop by drop, next to the tallest tree. He dug into the soil and was surprised to find that while the topsoil was nearly dry, there was an onion-shaped wet zone underground that kept the ground moist, with almost no surface evaporation. The dripping water was being stored and sucked up by the tree as needed.

The discovery got him thinking. Israel's farmers had long used flood irrigation to water their fields. Farmers built costly canals and trenches that were then inundated with water. The wastefulness of flood irrigation is obvious, especially in places where great effort and expense are needed to bring water from a source. Much of the flood irrigation water evaporates or drains away before it can be absorbed by the roots.

Simcha began testing the idea of drip irrigation. He discovered that localized drops by the root of a plant significantly decrease the amount of water needed, while also leading to increased yields. This began a decades-long journey of trial and error, as he tested various materials and water pressures that would allow an irrigation pipe to drip water at regular intervals. A worldwide rubber shortage during World War II saw the proliferation of plastics that were cheaper and more easily available. Simcha experimented with various widths, refining the friction and water pressure needed to create a healthy flow of water that both nourished the plant and conserved water. The result was an irrigation system he believed would save an enormous amount of water by using narrow plastic tubes to deliver water directly to the base of the plant.

It took years to refine the system, during which Simcha was primarily busy building Israel's national water infrastructure. Stubborn and determined, he was also a leading figure in an audacious plan to establish eleven new communities in the Negev in a single night. Ben-Gurion understood that if the Negev region remained a vast and largely empty wasteland, the British would exclude it from the partition plan being devised. In October 1946, the Jewish National Fund, the Jewish Agency, and the Haganah joined together to pull off the daring feat. Working under the cover of darkness, they built at least one structure with a roof in eleven predetermined locations across the Negev. Under British law, Jews were forbidden to establish new farms and settlements, but there was a loophole. An old Ottoman law was still in effect stipulating that no structure with a roof could be destroyed by the government unless it posed a safety hazard.

Simcha was responsible for ensuring the new communities had water. He helped select locations in places likely to have underground water or within a pipeline's distance from a source. He quietly arranged to purchase a large consignment of steel pipes from a source in London. During the war, a network of pipes was purchased and laid to put out fires caused by the Nazi blitz. Now that the war was over, the pipes were no longer necessary, and while the expense was high, Simcha used them to connect the new settlements to a water source.

One of the new communities was Kibbutz Hatzerim, located a few miles west of Beersheba. For several years, the farming community struggled with poor soil and parched land. The government encouraged the young pioneers to persevere, telling them that the community was important for Israel. In 1964, a new group of youngsters joined the community, including a twenty-year-old named Naty Barak. Born and raised in Haifa, Naty and his friends were young, idealistic, and committed to helping build the Jewish state.

Ben-Gurion was, at this time, imploring people to move south. He wrote, "It is absolutely vital for the State of Israel, for both economic and security reasons, to move southward: to direct the country's water and rain, the young pioneers and the new immigrants…to the south. We must concentrate the attention of Israel's scientists and research workers on the investigation of the forces, known or latent, with whose aid we shall be able to make the lands of the south and the Negev thrive."[50]

Naty and his friends answered Ben-Gurion's call to move south and settle in the Negev. "I saw it as an adventure," Naty recounts. "I dreamed about driving a tractor in the endless Negev, but the reality was that most of the time we were moving aluminum irrigation pipes with sprinklers." It was backbreaking work done in sweltering heat. Naty and his friends helped irrigate fields that grew cotton, sugar beets, corn, potatoes, and cucumbers. "We would wake up early, go to the dining room, then get a ride on a tractor out to a field, and spend a day moving the pipes." He recalls that "it gave me a lot of time to think." At the end of the day, everyone would gather at the public showers. "It was the center of information each day at four o'clock in the afternoon. We'd find out all the news and details of the day."

A year after he joined the kibbutz, a meeting was called to hear about a novel idea called drip irrigation. Simcha had been searching for a kibbutz to partner with him in manufacturing and marketing his invention, and Kibbutz Hatzerim was looking for a solution to its water challenges. Simcha had been

---

[50] Ben-Gurion, *Israel: Years of Challenge*, 201.

turned away by several kibbutzim because they didn't think his irrigation system would work. Kibbutz Hatzerim was willing to take a chance, and together they created a privately owned company called Netafim Irrigation Equipment & Drip Systems. In 1966, the company began manufacturing drippers and dripper lines, selling them first in Israel and later all over the world.

Today, Netafim works in 110 countries and has captured one-third of the global market share in drip irrigation. Thanks to their efforts, Israel is recognized as a world leader in producing new varieties of crops that require less water or less expensive water. The company's chief sustainability officer emeritus is none other than Naty Barak, who helped oversee the company's work with small-scale farmers in developing countries. "We are a private company," he reflects, "but we are doing well by doing good."

That motto still rings true today and is in keeping with the pioneering spirit and idealism of its early days. Ben-Gurion once wrote, "Israel has been granted a great, historic privilege, which is also a duty…to solve the gravest problems of the twentieth century—the dangerous gap between Asia and Africa, on the one hand, and Europe and America, on the other."

Ben-Gurion dreamed that the Jewish state would embody Jewish values. Again and again, the Torah implores to take special care of the vulnerable and lonely. From the prophecies of Amos to the Talmudic rulings that shape Jewish law, we are called upon to be global citizens who demonstrate moral concern for individuals and communities on the social margins. Call it חסד (*chesed*, or kindness) or תיקון עולם (*tikkun olam*, or the duty to better the world) or צדקה (*tzedakah*, or charity) or ואהבת לרעך כמוך (*ahavat l're'acha kamocha*, or love thy neighbor as thyself) or אור לגויים (*ohr lagoyim*, or a light onto the nations).

Whether spurred by obligation or impulse, helping others is central to Jewish identity and practice.

It's not surprising, then, that Jewish people building a Jewish state joined in global efforts to help humanity. Israel's founders understood the importance—politically, economically, and morally—to reach beyond their own borders and help others. In achieving sovereignty, they earned the instruments and institutions to extend our moral universe and improve the condition of peoples and nations fighting to break free from poverty. Israel gave birth to a new type of Jew—independent and confident—able both to take care of the Jewish people and to contribute to the improvement of the overall global condition.

"Seeds are the basis for food in the world, but the best seeds were not getting to the hungriest countries."

—Shoshan Haran

Fair Planet

I interviewed Shoshan Haran on January 2, 2023.

On October 7, 2023, sixty-seven-year-old Shoshan Haran was abducted to Gaza by Hamas; the family's home on Kibbutz Be'eri was found empty and burned beyond recognition. Shoshan's husband, Avshalom Haran, was murdered as were Shoshan's sister Lilach Kipnis and Lilach's husband, Eviatar.

Six of Shoshan's close relatives were also abducted: Shoshan's daughter Adi and her husband, Tal, and their two children; and Avshalom's sister Sharon Avigdori and her daughter Noam.

After enduring fifty days in captivity in Gaza, Shoshan was released with her daughter and grandchildren. Sharon and Noam were also released.

As of the time of publication, Tal Shoham was still being held as a hostage in Gaza.

Nearly 690 million people, or about 9 percent of the people on our planet, go to bed hungry each night.[51] The situation is expected to worsen as the world's population grows to an anticipated 10 billion people by 2050. Farmers will need to produce about 70 percent more food than they do presently to satiate a growing and hungry planet.

Agriculture is the main source of sustenance for hundreds of millions of people around the world who struggle with poverty and hunger. Most farmers operate on a minuscule scale: their plots of land are no larger than the size of a soccer pitch. In sub-Saharan Africa and South Asia, these farmers collectively supply most of the population's food. But it isn't enough. Beyond growing populations and increasingly unpredictable climate variability and extremes, as well as desertification, mean that current farming practices are falling short of producing a reliable and sufficient source of food. Hunger and malnutrition are linked to poverty, which in turn is linked to health, education, and economic and social development.

When Dr. Shoshan Haran started thinking deeply about this problem, the solution seemed obvious. "Seeds are the basis for food in the world, but the best seeds were not getting to the hungriest countries," she explains.

Having spent most of her life on and around farm fields, Shoshan should know. She grew up in Be'eri, a kibbutz that her parents helped found in southern Israel with its fourteen

---

[51] Food and Agriculture Organization of the United Nations, *The State of Food Security and Nutrition in the World, 2020*, https://www.fao.org/3/ca9692en/online/ca9692en.html#chapter-Key_message.

hundred hectares of field crops. After studying plant protection at the Hebrew University of Jerusalem, she returned to Kibbutz Be'eri to work in its cotton fields; raised her children; completed a PhD in plant sciences; and earned a two-year Fulbright postdoctoral fellowship to research plant-based pharmaceuticals at Rutgers University. An admitted plant-science nerd, Shoshan took her impressive credentials and joined Israel's largest seed-breeding company, Hazera (Hebrew for "seed"), where she oversaw R&D collaborations and intellectual property.

The global seed industry is on a continuous mission to design seeds that can produce more and better food. Investments in the science of these seeds are enormous. As Shoshan explains, "Typically, R&D investments are between 15 percent to 20 percent of a company's global income, amounting to billions of dollars invested every year to develop new and better plant varieties. R&D is tremendously expensive and time-consuming. It can take as much as eight to ten years to develop a new seed variety."

Since the goal is to encourage innovation that will improve food production, the seed industry has a unique approach to intellectual property. A plant-breeding exemption allows breeders to legally build on the work of others. Say, for example, a breeder from one company develops a new tomato variety that produces more tomatoes per plant. Competitor breeders are allowed to take that higher-yielding tomato plant variety and add their own improvements, such as a variety that produces firmer tomatoes. The result is an even better-quality plant built on the work and investments of others.

Billions of dollars and years of investments mean the global seed companies have amassed an impressive collection of high-quality seeds that yield bigger harvests, are more resistant to insect pests and diseases, better tolerate drought or flood, and have a greater ability to thrive in challenging climates and conditions.

As she pored through strategy documents, forecasts, and growth plans, Shoshan was struck by the fact that it was usually only large-scale farmers in developed countries who had access to high-quality seeds. The problem was glaring. "Because the R&D costs are so high for high-quality seeds," Shoshan says, "they become out of reach for the millions of small-scale farmers in low-income countries."

According to the World Bank, seed is the most important input in crop production.[52] The notion that warehouses were holding high-quality seeds while people were going hungry troubled Shoshan. Something needed to be done to connect the best seeds in the world with the poorest farmers. Years in academia had prepared her to undertake exhaustive research. To her mind, the problem was obvious, but she admits there was a lot she didn't know about devising solutions. For a start, she had never been to an African country, but that was easily remedied. She convinced her friend Amnon Tamir to join her on a trip to Kenya and Ethiopia to meet with small-scale farmers, agricultural companies, and government officials.

The on-the-ground experience provided a host of revelations. From her years on Kibbutz Be'eri and at Hazera, Shoshan had a solid understanding of the business model for selling high-quality seeds in high-income countries. Seed companies approach farmers and offer samples of a new seed variety. The farmer allocates a small plot next to an existing variety to see

---

[52] World Bank, *Enabling the Business of Agriculture, 2017: Seed,* https://thedocs.worldbank.org/en/doc/548701534213558444-0050022018/original/EBA17Seed.pdf.

how the new seed fares. If there is improved yield, quality, or nutritional values—factors that lead to higher profits—the farmer places an order for the new seeds.

This model wouldn't work in Kenya or Ethiopia. For one, small-scale subsistence farmers often live hand-to-mouth. They have very small plots of land and grow just enough food to feed their families. The yields are low and the vulnerability to climate impact is high. More importantly, they had no means to acquire higher-quality seeds. The fact that many farmers lived in remote locations and a large percentage of them were illiterate further complicated matters.

It also became clear that simply handing out high-quality seeds wouldn't be enough. For farmers to truly succeed, they would need to properly prepare their land, select crop varieties based on their suitability to local conditions, and then protect the young plants from pests and diseases as they grew. Shoshan and Amnon were struck both by the complexity of the challenges and the enormity of the need. Over seven million people suffer from malnutrition in Ethiopia, contributing to more than 50 percent of all infant and child deaths.[53] The reality was that to increase food security, farmers needed to dramatically increase their crop yields.

Shoshan and Amnon returned home determined to tackle the challenges. First that meant convincing several seed companies to join the effort by sharing their seeds and the accompanying proprietary knowledge of how to grow them successfully.

"I knew it wouldn't make economic sense for seed companies to develop new varieties of seeds for small-scale farmers in Africa," Shoshan acknowledges, "but I also knew that it wasn't

---

53 World Food Programme, *WFP Ethiopia Country Brief, October 2022*, https://reliefweb.int/report/ethiopia/wfp-ethiopia-country-brief-october-2022.

necessary. The industry had already developed a huge collection of varieties for diverse agri-climates, so all we had to do was figure out which existing varieties would fit the needs of local farmers. A plant doesn't care if it's planted in the Netherlands or in Ethiopia. It grows according to the local climatic conditions."

To get the seed companies on board, Shoshan presented a plan that offered a win-win opportunity. If the companies donated high-quality seeds to subsistence farmers, more farmers would be able to feed their families and begin to accumulate savings. Once the farmers earned greater economic independence, they would be able to purchase seeds, which would open new markets for the seed companies. Shoshan arranged a meeting with the head of strategy for the international seed cooperative that had purchased Hazera. The meeting was a success, and, impressed with Shoshan's vision, the company agreed to share some of its seeds and proprietary knowledge.

With a commitment secured from one of the world's largest seed companies, Shoshan quit her job in 2012 and founded Fair Planet. The name was chosen to reflect her belief that every farmer matters. Fair Planet's mission is to help small-scale farmers in low-income countries exit the cycle of hunger and poverty by enabling access to high-quality seeds and better farming practices. Shoshan's vision was to catapult farmers from subsistence farming to running successful agribusinesses that would generate savings and lead to new economic opportunities.

With a nonprofit in place and seeds committed, Shoshan needed someone who could develop test fields where they would plant different seed varieties and work out which grew best in each region. A friend named Dr. Alon Haberfeld came to mind, but the trouble was that Shoshan didn't have the funds to provide a salary. Even so, she prepared a pitch and asked Alon to lunch. The food hadn't even arrived before Alon agreed to join Fair Planet and work for free.

For the first three years, Shoshan, Alon, and Amnon built Fair Planet without taking any payment. Bit by bit they convinced more seed companies to partner with them while searching for the right pilot community. Opportunity knocked when a friend of Shoshan's, who also happened to be the agricultural attaché for MASAHV in Addis Ababa, Ethiopia, visited Israel. After Shoshan explained the model to him, he suggested Fair Planet pilot its work in Butajira, three hours from the capital of Addis Ababa and where MASHAV was running a training program for avocado farmers. Fair Planet had secured the operational and legal framework to set up its first test field in a developing country.

Once on the ground in Ethiopia, Shoshan and Alon began experimenting. They knew they couldn't expect a seed variety that grew well in a controlled greenhouse in Israel to perform the same way in an open field in Ethiopia. Setting up a test field allowed them to plant a variety of seeds and determine which performed best under local conditions. Ethiopia has three main agri-climates—in the lowlands, midlands, and highlands. There is also a wet season and a dry season to account for. Fair Planet needed to determine which variety of seeds produced optimal results in each agri-climate and at different times of the year. After a little experimentation they had it figured out. In their first season, the yield of many tomato varieties was more than five times higher than the local average. Fair Planet had created a successful proof of concept.

Shoshan and Alon turned their attention to a new challenge. They would need to train local, small-scale farmers using only tools and techniques that the farmers could easily replicate and afford. For example, in Israel drip irrigation is ubiquitous because its highly effective. At the same time, it's costly and requires intensive and expensive maintenance. "One of the reasons a lot of aid programs fail is they try a copy-paste approach," Shoshan points out. "You can't expect that what works in one country or in one's place will automatically work in another. We needed to adapt our knowledge to local economic and technical capacities."

Shoshan asked Erez Gozan, one of Israel's leading vegetable growers, to join her in Ethiopia to study local farming practices and then develop crop-production guidelines that blended the best of Israeli agricultural knowledge with the capacities of local farmers. Erez did just that, working with local volunteers to find creative ways to instruct farmers. They saw, for example, that water- and soda-bottle caps are cheap and easily accessible, so Erez's guide instructs farmers on how much fertilizer to use, using the bottle caps as measurement tools.

Fair Planet spent considerable time researching local conditions and traditions. They learned that in Ethiopia, locals don't want to buy round tomatoes. The preference is for elongated tomatoes. That's an important factor in selecting tomato varieties and planting with an eye toward market demand. On the other hand, they took note of farming practices that were hindering the success of many farmers. Many Ethiopian farmers allow weeds to grow wild in their fields, believing that the weeds were protecting their crops. In fact, weeds steal water and fertilizer from plants and serve to incubate pests and diseases.

Fair Planet needed a model to provide ongoing training to local farmers. Shoshan struck on the idea to replicate what Israel had done in its earliest years, when it was still a developing country. In the 1950s, thousands of Jews arrived in Israel, most of whom knew very little about agriculture. Israel sent the few agricultural experts they had to the farms all over the country to teach them how to farm. The early pioneers learned by doing. The method proved so successful that Israel continues to use it today. When Shoshan was working in the cotton fields of Kibbutz Be'eri, she was visited every week or two by experts from Shaham, the extension arm of the Israeli Ministry of Agriculture. Agronomists from Shaham walked with Shoshan through the kibbutz fields, taught her to identify pests and diseases, and explained how to treat them. It was hands-on training that stood the test of time.

Shoshan set up a similar model in Ethiopia. Fair Planet partnered with the local bureaus of agriculture and, together with their extension teams, identified lead farmers in the villages where they were working. Lead farmers were early adapters who were keen to share knowledge and best practices with their neighbors. They were given samples of high-quality seeds, received intensive training, and were then visited on their farms each week by expert agronomists.

"It's time-consuming and intensive effort," Shoshan admits, "but it works. When an expert walks through the fields with a local farmer, she can point out if the soil is too wet or too dry. She can look at the leaves and identify if there is a disease that needs to be addressed. She can see if the plants are getting too much sun or not enough. And so on."

Visiting experts offer instructions on every dimension of farming, including the conditions that maximize productivity. Crop rotation, for example, dictates that a farmer should not repeatedly grow the same crop in a field. For one, they need to give the soil the chance to replenish key nutrients. Second, every crop has specific pathogens. When a farmer grows a crop, say for example tomatoes, there are pests in the soil that attack their roots. The first time they encounter tomato roots, there aren't many soil-borne diseases, but they build up as the season progresses. If the farmer plants tomatoes again in the same field, the incubated pathogens attack, and that leads to a lower yield. By the third season, the plants start to suffer significantly. Farmers need to rotate between botanical families to keep ahead of the pathogens. For instance, tomatoes and peppers are from the same botanical family, so a farmer shouldn't plant them in succession. They can switch to cabbages or onions, which are in different botanical families and will suppress the tomato-plant pathogens.

Many of the farmers grew plants in pools of water, using a technique called flooding irrigation. The still water attracts diseases and causes the plants to rot, so visiting experts introduced farmers to furrow irrigation, a method of creating water channels in the soil so gravity plays the role of providing just enough water for plants to grow.

The results speak for themselves. Once lead farmers saw the improved yield, quality, and profit, they were eager to continue utilizing high-quality seeds and new farming techniques. Their success motivated their neighbors to follow suit and adopt new practices.

Today, Fair Planet has expanded operations to Tanzania and Rwanda, and it partners with nine of the largest seed companies in the world and runs five training centers. In Ethiopia, where operations began, Fair Planet has engaged over two hundred volunteers to educate over seventy-five thousand farmers across the country. Thanks to the rapid adoption of high-quality seeds and improved farming practices, these farmers have tripled their food production. More importantly, 91 percent sold most of their produce, and 96 percent benefitted from improved nutrition.

When evaluators asked the families how they were using the extra income, almost half reported that they were sending their children to school. Since only about half of the surveyed farmers had school-age children, it meant that almost all the farmers with young children were able to give them an education. An astounding 96 percent of farmers reported they were able to save money. The Fair Planet vision is materializing as entire communities transition from growing just enough to feed their families to breaking free from the cycle of poverty.

"These diseases are not only a medical problem but also a social and economic problem."

—Zvi Bentwich

NALA

In 2017, less than half of the global population had access to essential health services.[54] With more than one billion people living on less than one dollar per day and another two billion living on less than two dollars a day, health services are out of reach for huge swaths of the global population. Malnutrition and food insecurity weaken the immune systems, leaving people more susceptible to diseases. From there the situation spirals. Repeated and prolonged illnesses keep children out of school and prevent parents from being able to work, while the costs of obtaining health care can send a family into debt. A grinding

---

[54] World Bank, *Good Health and Well-Being: Why It Matters, 2020*, https://www.un.org/sustainabledevelopment/wp-content/uploads/2017/03/3_Why-It-Matters-2020.pdf.

cycle of poverty traps generation after generation in a perpetual and desperate loop. Curing and preventing the diseases of poverty is essential to fighting poverty itself. In the world's poorest countries, HIV, tuberculosis, diarrheal diseases, and malaria are killers.

Not that long ago, malaria plagued the region in which Israel finds itself. During World War I, malaria hounded General Allenby's Egyptian Expeditionary Force in Palestine. "This is one the most malaria-afflicted countries in the world," wrote Allenby's chief medical officer. In British-ruled Palestine, it killed thousands of people each year, and as much as 20 percent of the population was estimated to have contracted the disease. Pioneering Jews purchased plots of land to settle the country, but the land they could afford was often waterlogged marshes riddled with malaria-carrying mosquitoes. Entire regions had to be abandoned due to the high prevalence of the disease.

A physician immigrant named Dr. Hillel Yaffe made it his mission to tackle the malaria epidemic in service of the Zionist project and became a pioneer in malaria research. To reduce the prevalence of the deadly disease, he advised the city of Hadera to plant a eucalyptus forest to drain the swamps that served as mosquito-breeding grounds and to spray swamp lands with oil to interfere with the incubation of mosquitoes. To treat patients infected with the disease, Hillel introduced systematic use of the drug quinine, made from the bark of the South American cinchona tree.

Combined with a general improvement in public health under the British Mandate, the results were striking. In Jerusalem, according to British statistics, 633 people were treated for the disease in 1923. The following year, the number had dropped to 347. By 1928, the number was just 16. Land that had once been considered barely habitable could finally be settled.

Even as cases dropped, the fear of malaria kept people from moving to regions once plagued by the disease. To prove that taking quinine would keep the disease at bay, Dr. Yaffe moved with his wife and baby son to live in Hadera, offering bold proof of his faith in science.

Around the same time, a man by the name of Zvi Herbert Bentwich was making his own contribution to the Zionist cause in London, England. An acquaintance of Theodor Herzl and attendee at the first Zionist Congress in Basel, Herbert was one of the leaders of the British Jewish Zionist movement. He put his legal credentials to work by helping register the charter of the Zionist movement in Britain. In 1900, he planned a tour with British Zionists to the Holy Land, during which he befriended the renowned Dr. Yaffe. Their children, Sarah Yaffe and Joseph Bentwich, would eventually marry. The young, idealistic couple committed themselves to the Zionist dream, so Joseph gave up his position as a mathematician in Cambridge and moved to British-administered Palestine in 1924. A decade later, they gave birth to a son and named him Zvi after his grandfather.

In 1947, a twelve-year-old Zvi sat with his mother listening to the radio broadcast of the UN vote on November 29. "It was one of the most impressive, dramatic memories I have," he recalls. "Everybody was tense. I am not exaggerating in saying that the joy and celebration that night was unbelievable. People flocked to the streets singing, dancing, and climbing on top of cars." The euphoria lasted just one day because, as Zvi explained, "The following day war had broken out. My father was still working for the Mandate in charge of all Jewish education. He traveled to Tel Aviv for a meeting and couldn't return for a month because Jerusalem was under siege."

For months, families like Zvi's lived with the constant threats of Jordanian shelling, snipers, and the limited supplies of food and fuel that could be brought into Jerusalem. In May 1948, while living in Jerusalem under siege, Ben-Gurion proclaimed the State of Israel. Zvi listened in rapt attention to the radio once again. A few months later, during an agreed-upon thirty-day truce between Israel and the Jordanians, the Bentwich family was finally able to leave Jerusalem and resettle in Haifa, accompanied by Zvi's maternal grandmother. With her influence in the home, Zvi jokes that he was destined to become a physician. "My grandmother probably brainwashed me to be like my grandfather because she lived with us. At nine, I already was saying I wanted to be a doctor."

Sure enough, Zvi studied medicine at the Hebrew University and, after completing his military service as a flight surgeon in the air force, settled into life as a physician and discovered a particular interest in immunology. He rose through the ranks, spending time at the Weizmann Institute and Rockefeller University, until he was appointed head of the Department of Medicine at Kaplan Medical Center in Rehovot, where he continued his clinical immunology research.

By the 1980s, Zvi was spending much of his time studying the AIDS epidemic. Fear directed much of how the public saw the disease, leading to terrible stigmatization of people who had contracted it. "It was called the 'homosexual disease,'" Zvi recalls, "and that discrimination and persecution was part and parcel of the impact of that disease." Following in the footsteps of his grandfather, who tackled both the science and stigma of malaria, Zvi made a point to lead by example. He cofounded the Israel AIDS Task Force and opened Israel's first AIDS clinic. There, while searching for a solution to the disease, he made a point to spend time with AIDS patients, caring for them and treating them with respect, while fighting the fear that was prevalent in the medical community and among the public.

When waves of Ethiopian immigrants arrived in Israel in the late 1980s, Zvi had already earned a reputation as the Israeli physician tackling the HIV/AIDS epidemic. He noticed that the new immigrants had an unusually high prevalence of HIV, more than tenfold that of the Israeli population. Intrigued, he also noted that in Western countries, it was mostly men who suffered from AIDS, but among the new Ethiopian immigrants, the rates were also high among women. That clue led him to a revelation. Most researchers were spending their time investigating the virus. Zvi struck on the idea to study the host. "I was interested to see if there was anything different in the immune system of the host." Given the high rates of the virus among African women, he guessed there might be other infections at play that were making the women more susceptible to HIV.

"Although immunologists knew parasites have an effect on the immune system, it hadn't been well researched," he recounts. "I began studying non-HIV positive immigrants and then conducted a series of studies showing that intestinal worms that most immigrants were infected with had produced a major effect on the immune system." Following this line of thinking, he discovered a correlation between people infected with intestinal worms and those with severely compromised immune systems caused by the AIDS virus. "It became clear that they had a high prevalence of these neglected tropical diseases. The obvious conclusion was that their immune systems were compromised by the worms, so they were more susceptible to AIDS and less able to cope with the disease."

With this mystery unlocked, Zvi knew that to fight AIDS, modern medicine needed to eradicate neglected tropical diseases, or NTDs. Over one billion people, or a quarter of the world's population, are afflicted with these diseases. NTDs encompass over twenty diseases common in the world's poorest communities, where it is hard to source clean water or safe ways to dispose of human waste. Untreated, these parasites and worms cause debilitating diseases.

"These diseases are not only a medical problem but also a social and economic problem," Zvi explains. There are the costs to the health system to provide medical treatment and limit the outbreak and spread of disease. First, a major outbreak can overwhelm health systems, limiting the capacity to deal with other health issues. Second, epidemics force both those who are sick and their caretakers to miss work or be less effective at their jobs, driving down productivity. Third, fear of disease can have negative harm by closing schools and businesses and limiting public services—all of which disrupt the economy of a society. "The solution," Zvi concludes, "has to come from teaching people how to avoid getting the worms. The cost to treat intestinal worms is just a few cents, but once the worms compromise someone's immune system and they contract more serious diseases, the treatment costs skyrocket."

Armed with this knowledge, Zvi set out on a personal crusade to eradicate intestinal parasitic infections. He reached out to the Ministry of Health in Ethiopia to initiate a broad public health campaign to combat NTDs. Interestingly, he wasn't the first in his family to provide assistance in Ethiopia. His paternal uncle, Norman Bentwich (eldest son of Herbert

Bentwich), was the first attorney general of Palestine under the British Mandate. He was instrumental in transforming the Ottoman legal system to the British judicial system under the Mandate, which is the basis of the Israeli judicial system to this day. During World War II, Norman Bentwich served as the personal advisor to Ethiopian Emperor Haile Selassie and offered help to the Ethiopian "lost" Jews, the Falashas. "He was considered by Ethiopian Jews as their personal messiah," Zvi shares. "Call it providence, if you like, that I found myself years later in a position to continue his work with the Ethiopian Jewish community."

In 2011, Zvi founded NALA to tackle the challenge. NALA is an acronym. The "N" stands for NTD (neglected tropical diseases). The other letters stand for "advocacy," "learning," and "action." The nonprofit focuses on the most prevalent NTDs: intestinal worms, schistosomiasis (also known as bilharzia), and trachoma, a disease of the eye caused by a bacterium, which is the world's leading cause of blindness.

Zvi observed that government agencies were running large public health campaigns to administer medications to treat NTDs, but as soon as people stopped taking the drugs, the diseases returned. To have a long-term and lasting effect, communities would need to adopt prevention mechanisms, and people would need to change their behaviors. That became NALA's primary mission, with Zvi regularly traveling between Israel and Ethiopia. The solution lies in educating communities about the prevention mechanisms that improve hygiene. NALA's approach may seem obvious—encouraging handwashing with soap, using the toilet rather than the field as a bathroom, and avoiding dirty water—but for there to be lasting change, communities need to change what they've been doing all their lives, and that's easier said than done.

Zvi's results speak for themselves. In 2009, 45 percent of school children in the Mekelle region in northern Ethiopia were infected with schistosomiasis and other intestinal parasites. Four years later, after NALA partnered with the community, the disease rate dropped to less than 2 percent, and most importantly, it stayed low.

This mission was continued by Michal Bruck, who took over as CEO of NALA in 2015. She spent her early twenties backpacking solo across Southeast Asia. Trekking through some of the world's poorest villages, she discovered that the tougher the economic situation, the more hospitable the community. "It was mind-blowing to see the generosity that people had, relative to the little that they had," she mused. "You learn that anywhere you go in the world, people can give, people can get, and they can partner."

Michal set her focus on sustainability, namely ensuring that partner communities in Ethiopia have the knowledge and means to combat NTDs. She helped NALA win a Bill and Melinda Gates Foundation Grand Challenges Explorations grant and expanded their work to Adwa, a town in northern Ethiopia. NALA hired local community leaders to integrate the program into the health and education systems, then partnered with the parent-teacher association to train college students, women's networks, school faculties, and even children, all with the aim of encouraging broad communal participation. These efforts led to a 60 percent reduction in NTD disease prevalence within a year and eventually a steady 90 percent reduction.

The enormous success prompted the Ethiopian government to invite NALA to partner in addressing the country's persistent hot spots where NTD rates remain high. Together, they codesign and pilot interventions with local partners on the ground, and when the model has proven successful, they hand it off to the community to run the project on their own. Thanks to these partnerships, millions of Ethiopians are living free of NTDs, and NALA has earned global recognition for community mobilization and leading behavioral change interventions.

At the age of eighty-seven, Dr. Zvi Bentwich makes clear that he is not interested in retirement. He volunteers his time each month treating Palestinians in villages and refugee camps across the West Bank, while keeping his sights on an even bigger challenge—eliminating debilitating NTDs in Ethiopia. With all that, he still finds time to ride his bicycle to the Tel Aviv beach every day.

"The solution is simple because the technology exists."

—Sivan Ya'ari

Innovation: Africa

Sivan Ya'ari confronted real poverty for the first time at the age of twenty. Born in Israel to an Algerian father and Tunisian mother, she had voluntarily completed her service in the Israel Defense Forces and was looking for a job. She met one of the owners of Jordache Jeans, and he took note of Sivan's fluency in French and asked if she'd be interested in overseeing quality control in his factory in Madagascar.

Arriving on the East African island nation, Sivan's perspective on poverty changed dramatically. Growing up in Israel, her father was frequently unemployed, and the family learned to make do. "I had always thought of my family as poor," Sivan says. "But I had shoes, I had a bed, I had access to electricity and water. In Madagascar, I spent a lot of time with women and children from a nearby village. One night, they took me to a medical center that had no electricity, where I saw women waiting to give birth in complete darkness. The only light was a candle and a small kerosene lamp."

Dismayed by what she'd witnessed, she learned that electricity isn't just about having light or heat. Two and half billion people around the world don't have access to energy. Without electricity, clinics can't store lifesaving vaccines and medications, children can't study at night or get an education on days when the sun isn't shining, and it's difficult to attract quality doctors or schoolteachers to communities without electricity.

The more she dug into the problem, the more Sivan believed that electricity could be a game changer for rural communities. She enrolled in a master's program at Columbia University to study energy management, and the coursework reinforced what she had seen firsthand: without energy, it is very difficult to have any kind of development, be it human or economic.

Equally importantly, Sivan learned that while there are an estimated four hundred million people in Africa who don't have access to clean water, there is plenty of clean water on the African continent. The challenge is that it is hidden in aquifers thirty to one hundred meters underground, far too deep to access manually. To bring the water to the surface, they need energy for pumps.

Installing pumps in rural communities would positively impact the lives of millions of people, who spend hours each day searching for surface water and wood that can be used as fuel to boil the water. Instead, they'd be able to pump clean water from aquifers to drink, cook, and grow food. When communities have access to clean water, people are healthier, children are more likely to attend school, women have the time to find new sources of income for their families, and businesses are created by entrepreneurs growing and selling food.

As a first-year graduate student, Sivan interned with the United Nations Development Program (UNDP). They were sending students to villages in Senegal to assess a program providing generators to communities. "Our job was to make sure that everything was working," Sivan says. "What we found was that most of the generators were not working. Either there was not enough fuel and the villagers didn't have money to buy more, or the generators broke and no one knew how to fix them."

Those were valuable lessons as she considered how she could help bring electricity to rural Africa. Her mind kept returning to her own experience growing up in Israel, where solar panels can be found on nearly every home to heat hot water. There is no more abundant and reliable source of free energy on the African continent than the sun. Sivan wondered if solar energy, which is simple to set up and inexpensive to generate, could be the solution.

She decided to test the idea with a pilot project to bring solar panels to Kidegozero Health Center in Tanzania. Still a graduate student, Sivan founded a nonprofit and gave it the name Jewish Heart for Africa. Together with just one local contractor, they installed two solar panels on the roof of a medical clinic. The result was transformative. Sivan proudly exclaims, "For the first time, nurses could take care of patients in the evening without using candles for light. There was also a refrigerator that keeps the vaccines and drugs from spoiling."

Having created a successful proof of concept, Sivan expanded her efforts village by village. The one snag she kept encountering was the name of her organization, Jewish Heart for Africa. Villagers were wary of the strangers who arrived, convinced they were trying to convert them to Judaism. Sivan did her best to explain that their only intention was to share Israeli solar technology, but she finally relented and changed the name of the nonprofit to Innovation: Africa. Sivan added the tagline: *Bringing Israeli innovation to African villages.*

Innovation: Africa focuses its efforts on truly remote communities deep in the countryside that are typically a ten-to-eighteen-hour drive away from urban centers. These villagers have mostly never heard of Israel, and if they have, it's from the Bible.

To hear Sivan describe it, bringing solar power and clear water to the most remote parts of Africa sounds straightforward. It's obviously not, but Sivan is a sunny optimist whose mottoes are "One step at a time" and "Focus on the journey, not the destination." She frequently reminds her staff to avoid getting stuck on the "Why?" and instead relentlessly pursue the "How?"

Sivan admits that she has failed many times since she started out in 2008, but each failure brought new insights and lessons. Early on, she learned that the key to success is to work with the target community from day one and to be mindful and respectful of local customs and culture. They learned this lesson the hard way. In one of the first villages where they installed solar energy at a school, Sivan returned after a few months and saw that while the solar system was operating, the students and teachers refused to use it, because they were convinced the light would attract witches to their school.

Sivan took the lesson in stride and has since spent more time with partner communities ensuring they understand every step of the process. "Let's say we want to work in Malawi," Sivan says. "We meet with the ambassador of Malawi at the UN. He introduces us to the relevant ministers, and then we meet with the minister of energy, the minister of health, the minister of agriculture, and so forth. We try to understand the country and find out where there is the most need. Specifically, we look for districts that are remote from the grid. I'm talking about places that won't get electricity for at least the next twenty years."

Next, they check that the local community is willing to take ownership of the project. "Choosing the right villages is not simple," Sivan admits. "You have to work with the local government, ministers, district officers, as well as the chiefs of the villages and the community members to identify communities most in need of our assistance. Once our team confirms that a village fits our criteria, we spend a lot of time with the community to ensure they are fully engaged and a solar or water committee is appointed. This committee will help ensure the successful implementation of the project and its long-term success."

Innovation: Africa hires civil and electrical engineers, hydrogeologists, and various energy and water experts. Ninety-five percent of the project's costs are purchased locally, which provides an economic injection into the community. For each project, they hire ten local villagers who are trained and work with the contractor for three months. Those villagers learn all aspects of the project and acquire the skills to maintain and repair all the equipment. Only then does the team begin drilling, sometimes as far down as 250 meters, and installs a water pump, which propels the water up from the aquifer and into the 10,000-liter tank that is raised onto the 10-meter tower. The solar panels installed on top of the tower harness the energy from the sun to power the pump. One solar water pumping system can provide enough water for up to 10,000 people.

Next, the Innovation: Africa team erects an enormous water tank atop a tall tower where groundwater is pumped and stored for distribution. They dig kilometers of trenches around the village to lay pipes that will distribute water throughout the community, providing clean water for washing, drinking, and food preparation. Often, another water pump is installed and connected to a drip-irrigation system that was also invented in Israel. Using this system enables villagers to grow more food using a smaller amount of water. It also means they are less dependent on rainwater, because they can access the water in the aquifer and in the water tank.

The Innovation: Africa engineering team developed an "Energy Box" that has the capacity to light an entire school and medical center from a single system. They use lithium-ion batteries and special LED light bulbs that are made in Israel and can last fifty thousand hours. This creates sustainability and efficiency while being cost-effective. The solar and water infrastructure installed in each village is designed to last for decades. To ensure everything is working optimally, they also install remote monitoring technology. Each unit sends information to a server that measures how much solar energy is produced and consumed, as well as how much water is being pumped at any given time. This allows a team to ensure that the systems are operating correctly, and should a malfunction occur, an alert is sent to a local engineer who can investigate.

With each project, Sivan is bringing a little bit of Israeli ingenuity to light up a community.

"It's all right there," she says proudly. "Israel is such a small country, and yet it has produced so much innovation in such a short time. It's only in recent years that we have become stable enough and strong enough to begin to fulfill our destiny and do what we are meant to do, and that is to share and help others."

Innovation: Africa has brought solar technologies to five million people in over one thousand villages across ten African countries: South Africa, Eswatini, Uganda, Malawi, Tanzania, Zambia, Cameroon, Democratic Republic of Congo, Senegal, and Ethiopia. The impact has been profound. Once lights are installed in school, more children graduate. Once medical clinics have electricity and refrigeration, more doctors are prepared to work in rural villages. Once women don't have to spend time searching for water and fuel, they can earn an income to support their families. In some communities, local women create small businesses using surplus energy created by the solar panels. One popular endeavor is to provide a charging station for cell phones. People from surrounding villages pay ten to fifteen cents to charge their cell phones. A portion becomes a small income for the business owners, and the rest is deposited in a bank account to pay for replacement light bulbs and batteries when they are needed.

Sivan has big dreams. She is determined to bring electricity and clean water to ten million people by the end of 2026. "We can do it," she insists. "We can bring water where there is drought, light where there is darkness, and dignity where there is despair. The solution is simple because the technology exists. And the impact is priceless."

"We Israelis assume there is always a way."

—Jacob Sztokman

Gabriel Project Mumbai

India is a country of extreme contrasts in wealth. Metropolitan areas like Mumbai, Delhi, and Bangalore boast a growing number of billionaires. At the same time, 60 percent of the country's nearly 1.4 billion people live on less than $3.10 a day, the World Bank's median poverty line. Poverty, illiteracy, and malnutrition go hand in hand. Poor children in India are three times more likely to die than children anywhere else in the world. About 7 million Indian children live in slums without access to an education. Since food is scarce and families struggle to survive, there is tremendous pressure on children to work. Slum children as young as four or five years old work in menial jobs, such as ragpickers or sewage cleaners, earning a few cents a month to stave off their families' hunger.

The Kalwa slum, on the outskirts of Mumbai, is home to an estimated 180,000 people. It has no plumbing or sewage system and limited access to water, electricity, and sanitation. Walking through the slum, it can take a moment to find one's bearings and absorb the scene. Heaps of trash as high as one- or two-story buildings line the sides of the road, and atop them pigs root for food. A putrid smell wafts from a thick, murky waterway choked by all manner of litter. The dirt roads are pocked with litter and lined with single-room, cinder-block homes. Some are covered in sheets of tin, while others have little more than tarps to protect from the sun and monsoons. On the streets, motorcycles and handcarts carry goods every which way. The odd goat ambles by, unperturbed by the local hustle and bustle. People carry jerry cans or sit outside little shops with brightly colored signs watching the passersby. Most residents pay no attention to visitors. A few women in tidy, colorful saris offer a shy smile, but the children wave exuberantly and demand high fives.

It was the children who captured Jacob Sztokman's heart and led him to found Gabriel Project Mumbai (GPM), an NGO caring for vulnerable children and their communities in slums and underserved rural villages across India.

In 2011, Jacob—who was born in Australia and moved to Israel in his twenties—was working in Israel's fast-paced high-tech scene and arrived in India for the first time on a ten-day business trip. "India wasn't even on my radar. I didn't even like Indian food," he says with a wry smile. "Each afternoon I would go for a walk, and I soon found that any ten-minute walk in Mumbai led to a slum. I knew about India's poverty challenges, but it was shocking to see it firsthand. Children were eating from mounds of garbage and working as sewage cleaners." Shaking his head, he continues, "It's one thing to know poverty exists out there, and it's another thing to see it up close."

Jacob returned to Israel, but he couldn't stop thinking about the children. He had a nagging feeling that something needed to be done, and he would lie awake at night tormented by the notion that he should help. The grandson of Holocaust survivors, Jacob had grown up hearing about the absolute moral imperative to address human suffering.

The trouble was, Jacob didn't know the first thing about international development.

"That was my first visit. I knew nothing about the culture or the language, so I read up," Jacob says. "Then I went back to India twice on my own dime to speak with NGOs and see if there was a gap I could help fill." He thinks back to those early years and adds, "Maybe I was being naïve. But my wife was very supportive. She was willing to be the sole provider for a while, and I wanted my children to be proud of me." He pauses. "There were lots of people, including in my family, who told me I was crazy to think I could make a difference. But I'm proudly Israeli, and we Israelis assume there is always a way."

Those trips cemented his determination. Less than a year after he traveled to India for the first time, he quit his job and founded GPM. The name is a tribute to Jacob's grandfather, Gabriel, and in memory of Gavriel Holtzberg, the Israeli Chabad rabbi murdered in the brutal 2008 Mumbai terrorist attack.

GPM began with a simple idea. Jacob would partner with an education NGO working in Kalwa slum and provide meals for the five hundred children in their school. For many of those children, it was the only food they would eat all day.

Jacob had never run a nonprofit or fundraised. As he navigated the complexities of running an organization, he dove into the world of international development best practices and enrolled in a master's program. The more he learned, the more Jacob felt he should take GPM in a new direction. He felt the education being provided to the children was lacking, so he turned his attention to understanding India's education system and the pedagogy of early childhood education. Determined to give the children in Kalwa the best possible education, GPM opened its own school, with a focus on teaching children to problem-solve and think creatively, rather than memorize.

Rather than rote memorization, GPM's teachers use games and activities to reinforce learning objectives. Before, if children were learning fractions, they would sit in their seats and repeat formulas drilled by the teacher. Now the kids were asked to stand and divide themselves in half. With a bit of instruction, they understood the concept. Next, they were asked to divide into thirds. Again, with some patience and practice, they soon understood what was being asked. In time, the concept of fractions became familiar, and they could apply logic to divide themselves into eighths or tenths or whatever fraction was asked by the instructor.

The two-story school building is bright and cheerful. Fans whirl in the corners and the walls are decorated with colorful posters, English vocabulary cards, and students' artwork, including a hand-drawn Israeli flag flanked by colorful paper dolls from around the world. While GPM is a secular organization, it is rooted in Jewish values of service and citizenship.

Jacob had the idea to recruit volunteers from the Mumbai Jewish community and from Jewish communities around the world to assist at GPM, while learning about international development, Indian culture, and the Jewish ethics of social justice. This too had a learning curve. The first time he went to rent an apartment in Mumbai to house overseas volunteers, he ran into trouble. He was all set for the arrival of four college students when the condo society contacted him and cancelled his rental. "When I asked why," he says, "they told me that they wouldn't be party to prostitution. No matter what I said, they just couldn't imagine any other reason for four college-age girls to be in a Mumbai apartment."

GPM has continued to provide nutritious meals for children who attend school. Each day, when lessons conclude, a small group of women arrive carrying trays of steaming hot food. Providing a hot and nutritious meal is often reason enough for parents to send their children to school rather than to work, and ensuring the children aren't hungry means that they can focus on learning.

Fortuitously, just as Jacob was launching GPM, he met a group of women who wanted to start a business to earn extra money for their families. Jacob hired them to cook the hot lunches. That lunch business grew to become the Masala Mamas catering business. Inside a small one-room kitchen, women dressed in colorful saris and ankle bracelets squat on the floor, working. They chat with one another as they wash rice, make chapatis, blend aromatic spices, and stir vats of spicy vegetable curries. There is no oven, and the kitchen doesn't always have running water or electricity, so the women cook on stoves, preparing cakes and breads in a pan. Despite the simplicity of the kitchen, Masala Mamas prepare meals for hundreds of children each day.

Most women in the Kalwa slum can't commute into the city of Mumbai to work a full day because they're expected to stay close to home and take care of their families. Many are illiterate, which further limits their employment opportunities. The result is that they are reliant on their husbands' income, which may not stretch to meet the needs of the family. GPM helps empower them through women-led social enterprises like Sundara, which is Sanskrit for "beautiful," and was founded by Boston-area native Erin Zaikis.

When *Slumdog Millionaire* came out in 2008, Erin was nineteen years old. After watching the film, she was gripped by the notion that there were children raising themselves in abject poverty. She wanted to understand how it was possible and what she could do. She spent her bat mitzvah savings to buy a flight ticket to India. In Mumbai, she lived and worked at Seva Sadan Society, an orphanage for girls abandoned as babies in trash cans and train stations because their parents couldn't afford to raise them. For Erin, their stories were a stark introduction to the realities of extreme poverty. Seva Sadan Society provided the girls with a safe environment, an education, and, when they were older, job training. During her time in Mumbai, Erin met Jacob through the local Mumbai Jewish community and was introduced to the work at GPM.

After graduation, she moved to Thailand and spent two years with an NGO committed to fighting the child-sex-trafficking industry. During her time traveling through Thailand, Erin was surprised to find that many teenaged children had never been introduced to handwashing and simply didn't know what soap was. The problem irked her, and during a period of convalescence from dengue fever, she spent hours online researching everything she could on soap. She learned that there is already more than enough soap in the world to provide for every person, and she wanted to find a way to encourage safe hygiene while helping women earn extra income to lift them out of poverty.

Erin applied for and was awarded $10,000 in a LinkedIn competition to launch a soap-recycling program in India. She reached out to Jacob at GPM for advice, and he convinced her to pilot the program in the Kalwa slum. With his help, Erin found a space to set up a workshop, hired three local women, bought a soap press and raw materials, and taught the women how to make soap. The finished bars were distributed for free to tribal communities across Maharashtra, where people live on less than a dollar a day.

The idea to recycle hotel soap came after Erin read that five million soap bars wind up in landfills every single day in the United States alone, most from the hotel industry. She approached hotels in Mumbai and asked them to donate the used bars of soap left by guests. In time, more and more hotels joined the effort, until over one hundred hotels were donating their used bars of soap. Within a few years, Erin had built a successful operation that she named Sundara, which was later taken over by GPM and renamed Sundar India. Erin, meanwhile, expanded operations to Myanmar and Uganda, and collaborated on partnerships in Rwanda and South Africa.

The COVID-19 pandemic hit hard, and Sundar India dropped to just eight employees in six months. As of 2023, operations were limited to the state of Maharashtra, where Sundar India hires at-risk women—mostly widows, victims of domestic violence, and single mothers—to transform used donated soaps from hotels in and around Mumbai into new bars of soap. The job provides the first regular stream of income for the women of Sundar India. Those funds enable them to buy healthy foods for their families, send their children to school, start new businesses, and help ailing parents.

Inside the tidy room that serves as Sundar India's workshop, Madhuri, the center supervisor and one of Erin's first hires, demonstrates the process. She scrapes off the outer layer of soap and soaks it in water to ensure it's clean. Next, she grates the soap using a simple cheese grater, creating huge bowls of white flakes. Then she mixes the flakes with water and places the mixture into a hand-operated compressing machine, which squeezes the flakes into a bar. With a flourish, she shows us the final product—tidy bars of soap perfumed with different scents, packaged in simple paper with a tagline, "Doing good is beautiful." In addition to selling some of the soaps to tourists, Sundar India sets aside most of the bars to distribute to children at over fifty schools in the area, along with free lessons on handwashing and hygiene.

Over the years, GPM has expanded its offerings. First, they tackled nutrition, then education, then livelihood projects. Jacob realized there was a fourth critical pillar for any community: health care.

The realization was born from tragedy. Shravan Shah was a bright eleven-year-old boy and star pupil in GPM's school. He studied hard and dreamed of breaking free from the dire poverty that afflicted his family. "That's what made it so out of character when he missed school for several days," Jacob recalls. "The teachers went looking for him and were heartbroken to learn that Shravan had developed a fever in the night and passed away. There was not one single doctor in Kalwa, a community of almost two hundred thousand people. And the parents couldn't do anything to save his life." Jacob shakes his head. "It hit us like a ton of bricks. What is the use of providing a good education and good nutrition if there isn't accessible health care for these children, because their parents need to walk through a monsoon or extreme heat for hours to find a doctor?"

Jacob raised the funds, and in 2014 GPM was able to open Shravan Health Clinic, named in memory of the child who inspired the facility. It was the slum's first community medical clinic, hiring local doctors to care for the sick, provide immunizations, and offer preventive checkups. While the clinic could run at no charge to patients, Jacob learned that it was better to set a price, because people were skeptical of the quality of service provided for free. Today, the price is set at a modest twenty rupees (about twenty-five US cents) to cover a patient's treatment for the entire course of illness. Anyone who can't afford the twenty rupees is told to pay when he or she can. GPM also opened a pharmacy on site to provide discounted medications.

The staff are trained to ensure that any patient who is given a prescription gets the necessary medication. "Sometimes, they try to tell us that they will get the drugs somewhere else. But that usually means they are too embarrassed to tell us they can't afford them," Jacob explains. "The staff gives them the medication and assures them that it's fine to pay later. Sometimes, months will pass, and they will come back to us with the rupees they owe. They try their best."

The GPM team began to hear reports from doctors that many people arrived with diseases that came from drinking unclean water. As is typical in Indian slums, residents of Kalwa pay to pump water to use for drinking, cooking, and bathing. Borewells are supposed to be dug fifty to seventy-five feet underground to access the clean water table and bypass the sewage that seeps into the ground. It's an expensive process, so the wells are sometimes only dug to fifteen feet, which would be acceptable if the water were boiled before use. Since the fuel needed to build a fire is expensive, though, many people were forgoing the process and drinking contaminated water.

With another critical need identified, GPM built a safe-water filtration plant named Jal Jeevan Hain, or "Water Is Life," in the slum to produce clean drinking water. The water is then sold at a price comparable to what people pay for borewell water. Today, one thousand families are using clean water, and waterborne diseases have decreased overall across Kalwa.

This focus on holistic interventions goes to the heart of how GPM operates. When Jacob began work in Kalwa slum, there were 120,000 people living in the area. Seven years later, the population had ballooned to 180,000. Kalwa, like many other slums in major cities, was experiencing a huge population explosion as people left the poverty of rural villages in search of better opportunities.

Each month, close to 40,000 people arrive in Mumbai alone. Most end up living on the streets or in makeshift tents until they can find the means to move to one of the slums. GPM responded by reaching out to local villages to provide the same four pillars needed for the success of any community: education, nutrition, health care, and livelihood programs.

Jacob related an incident that took place when he traveled to a particularly remote area called Palghar district, where locals rarely interacted with Westerners. Jacob and his team met with a group of farmers participating in their farming collective. "Their faces were blank as they looked at me," Jacob says. "I could feel that they were distrustful and that some were even looking at me with disdain." That is, until his staff introduced him as being from Israel. "Suddenly their faces became animated," he says with a laugh. "They began talking to each other, and the only word I understood was Israel, Israel, Israel." They knew all about the ways Israel could farm productively in arid conditions, and the reason they knew was that farmers from the district had been invited to participate in MASHAV training programs.

Ten years after its founding, GPM is educating 300 children, providing safe drinking water to 1,000 families, treating 1,200 patients in the health clinic each month, and providing livelihood projects to over 100 people. The ripple effects of these interventions have transformed the lives of untold numbers of people. GPM has helped create a self-sustaining ecosystem that returns ownership back to the community. Farmers supply the food used by Masala Mamas to cook meals for school children.

Those children are getting an education that gives them the chance to provide for their families and improve their futures. Since the community has ownership in the various projects, it has a means to generate income to independently sustain the health clinic, water-filtration plant, and school.

In spring of 2021, India was hit by a devastating wave of COVID-19 infections. Hospitals ran out of beds and critical supplies, contributing to the deaths of untold thousands of people. At its peak, daily cases surged to over four hundred thousand, the most of any country at any point during the pandemic. Major shortages of medical supplies and medical staff left health-care facilities overburdened and struggling to cope with the influx of cases. GPM teamed up with Israeli NGO IsraAID to support twenty government-run hospitals in Palghar, a rural district north of Mumbai serving a population of over four million people, most of whom are indigenous tribal communities. The two organizations raised the funds for the overwhelmed hospitals to fill staffing shortages and sent desperately needed personal protective equipment and medical supplies.

One of the biggest challenges was providing enough medical oxygen for the most at-risk patients as demand rose tenfold. Some hospitals posted "oxygen out of stock" signs, while others asked patients to search for treatment elsewhere. In the village of one of GPM's staff members, every second house had someone with a serious case of COVID-19. As news organizations published stories about patients dying from a lack of oxygen, GPM and IsraAID took matters into their own hands by building an oxygen plant and vaporizer unit to support lifesaving efforts for hundreds of critical care patients. Today, one of the district hospitals still runs the plant to supply oxygen to the thirty-bed hospital and ensure that they are prepared for any future crisis.

Jacob's Postscript

Every day, our 70 non-Jewish staff in India join a Zoom call at 9am to review organizational business. Every Friday since October 7, these Zoom meetings start with a minute of silence for the Israeli hostages still being held by Hamas terrorists followed by a short prayer for peace.

* * *

"By eighth grade, I was Jewishly literate and unafraid of police attack dogs and tear gas."

—Yossi Abramowitz

Captain Sunshine

Yossi Abramowitz is a man of many titles: a founding father of Israel's solar market, civil rights activist, pioneering environmentalist, peoplehood champion, journalist, investor, global social entrepreneur, three-time Nobel Prize nominee, and former candidate for president of the State of Israel. Yossi has a knack for sniffing out big ideas.

A child of the 1960s, Yossi was raised by parents who lived and breathed activism. His father shared stories of attending the March on Washington and hearing the Rev. Martin Luther King Jr. deliver his famous "I Have a Dream" speech. As an adult, Yossi made it a point to stand in the exact same spot where his father had stood during that famous speech at President Barack Obama's inauguration.

In the Abramowitz household, activism demanded self-sacrifice. When Yossi was just a baby, his father wrote his young son a goodbye letter before traveling to Mississippi to register Black voters and protest the murder of three civil rights workers by the Ku Klux Klan. He returned unharmed, and the trip became the stuff of family lore, leaving an impression on his son. Yossi's mother was similarly passionate about social justice and regularly took Yossi to political and environmental rallies. Once, she pulled him out of school to attend an underground training in the basement of a Boston church. They spent the day in civil disobedience training to protest the planned construction of a nuclear power plant.

At the age of five, his parents moved to Israel. It was 1969, and they were swept up in the post–Six Day War euphoria, when Israel, having defeated the armies of Egypt, Syria, and Jordan, seemed invincible. "Those were magical years in the Jewish psyche," Yossi remembers, smiling. "There was a feeling that history, if not God, was on our side. And whatever seems impossible, if it's good, is possible."

Three years later, the family returned to Boston so his father could pursue a PhD at Brandeis, but the temporary move became permanent when his parents divorced. The separation didn't dimmish each parent's commitment to providing their children with a good Jewish education and instilling in them a love of Israel and devotion to civil rights. After the divorce, his mom moved with her two sons to a hippie commune in Massachusetts and became ever more passionate about activism. "By eighth grade, I was Jewishly literate and unafraid of police attack dogs and tear gas," Yossi says.

It wasn't long before Yossi became an outspoken activist in his own right. At Boston University, where he majored in Jewish public policy, he was elected to the National Hillel Student Secretariat, and following graduation, chair of the World Union of Jewish Students (WUJS), where he led the international student movement on behalf of Soviet Jewry. Like his father, Yossi was willing to put himself in harm's way. He was arrested outside the Soviet embassy in Washington, DC, while protesting on behalf of "refusenik" Boris Lifshitz, a young engineering student from Leningrad. He later went on a two-week hunger strike on behalf of "Prisoner of Zion" Alexei Magarik, who was subsequently released and moved to Israel. Alexei was the last Prisoner of Zion in the USSR.

It wasn't Yossi's first hunger strike. He had previously done so to protest Boston University's investments in South Africa's apartheid regime. Around the same time, Yossi also led a four-day protest outside the university president's office and joined a 1987 trip to South Africa, where he vocally advocated for the abolition of apartheid. His exploits nearly earned him deportation. Instead, he was handed a banning order, which he proudly framed and hung on his wall.

Yossi brought the same fierce determination to the movement to help Yemenite and Ethiopian Jews immigrate to Israel. Over the years, he has organized demonstrations in twenty-three countries. On top of his civil rights efforts, he was an outspoken environmentalist long before the movement gained popularity. In fact, he's pretty sure he was the first person in Massachusetts to buy a hybrid car.

Boston University provided fertile ground to become an entrepreneurial advocate. It was also where he met his future wife, Susan Silverman, who matched his idealism and determination. She helped celebrate the end of a ten-day hunger strike by buying him a cake frosted with the word "Justice." Over the years, Susan has made her own name as an activist rabbi, author, and adoption advocate. The couple are observant Jews who are unafraid to challenge religious orthodoxy and the status quo. The family motto is "Don't be a schmuck."

By 1996, the couple were parents to two young girls and had launched a national Jewish parenting magazine called *Jewish Family & Life*. The inaugural edition featured Hillary Clinton writing about Esther from the Purim story as a role model and Steven Spielberg sharing his matzo brei recipe.

Around the same time, Yossi learned of the dire situation of a group of Ethiopian Jews. A friend told him that Jewish huts were being burned in the northern Ethiopian village of Buchara. Neighbors were confiscating land and cattle and chasing Jewish families away. The Israeli government wouldn't intercede until there was proof of the crimes.

Yossi volunteered to collect evidence. He bought a bullet-proof vest in Boston and flew to Gondar with an Israeli friend named Agaru, who had grown up in Buchara. They hired a driver with a four-wheel-drive Jeep and set off for the remote village. Two hours into the trip, the driver swerved off the road and into a ditch. Leaving the driver to solve the Jeep issue, Yossi and Agaru continued on foot to the village, where they found burned circles where there used to be Jewish huts.

As Yossi pulled out a camera to document the evidence, they looked up to discover a man pointing a gun at them. Wary of strangers, the man demanded to know who they were and why they were in the village. Yossi, thinking quickly, told them that he was recruiting for the circus and deftly pulled out a friend's business card. Unsure what to make of the strangers, the gun-wielding man led them to a nearby home to eat injera and talk. Eventually, he allowed them to take photographs before escorting them back to their Jeep, which was still in the ditch. By now the sun was setting, and ignoring the danger, Yossi and Agaru abandoned the Jeep to walk. To their enormous luck, an Ethiopian police patrol happened to pass by, and they hitched a ride to town. Safely in his hotel, Yossi called his editor at the *Forward* and dictated a story over the phone. The ensuing press created the public pressure needed to convince the Israeli government to allow eight thousand Ethiopian Jews to immigrate to Israel.

Susan was not impressed by Yossi's dangerous escapades. Instead of overseas missions, she proposed a new family mission—to adopt a child. Yossi didn't need any convincing and, having just visited Ethiopia, relayed the deep need he had witnessed. On the Jewish holiday of Purim, they learned about an orphaned baby boy in Ethiopia and agreed on the spot to adopt him. They named their son Adar, after the Jewish month in which Purim takes place. A few years later, Adar lobbied hard to have a brother who looked like him, and the family adopted a second Ethiopian boy whom they named Zamir.

By 2006, Yossi and Susan were parents to five energetic and precocious children. Feeling overwhelmed and looking for a way to gel as a family, Susan suggested they take a sabbatical trip to Israel. Yossi longed to live in Israel and was overjoyed. Susan added one condition: they would live in a remote community far from the population centers of Israel. It was a deliberate move to keep Yossi from diving into new projects.

As a teenager in Young Judaea, a Zionist youth movement, Yossi had volunteered at Kibbutz Ketura in Israel's Arava Desert. A religious pluralistic kibbutz founded by former Young Judaeans, Ketura is located in the southern part of the Arava, a long, narrow rift valley stretching from the Dead Sea to the Red

Sea. Yossi emailed a friend on the kibbutz and convinced them to host their family.

In August 2006, the family arrived at the kibbutz, exited the air-conditioned van that brought them from the airport, and were blinded by the blazing sun. The hyper-arid region is known for scorching hot summers with the temperature soaring over ninety degrees Fahrenheit. The intensity of the desert sun had Yossi convinced the community must run on solar energy. He was taken aback to learn that Israel was entirely dependent on fossil fuels, even though two-thirds of its territory is a sprawling, sun-drenched desert. "It was nuts," he recounts. "Israel is a leader in tech, and it had no solar power."

By his third day in Israel, and ignoring his promise to Susan, an idea took shape. Yossi was going to figure out how to harness the Arava sun to create a sustainable source of power. He rented an office at the Arava Institute for Environmental Studies on the kibbutz and brought in experts in solar energy. Everyone warned him that Israeli politics and bureaucracy were difficult enough to navigate, and they would be impossible for a newly arrived naive American.

The challenge was daunting. Producing solar energy at the time was more expensive than coal, and the electricity system of the country wasn't set up for collecting and distributing solar power. On top of it all, there were twenty-four government offices to navigate. Yossi wasn't deterred. "I thought, wait a second. I can get a Hebrew teacher out of solitary confinement in Siberia. I helped to get sanctions imposed on apartheid South Africa. Can't we change a few laws in our own country?"

Together with Ed Hofland from Kibbutz Ketura and New York–based businessman David Rosenblatt, they founded the Arava Power Company. They learned they would have to surmount one hundred statutory, regulatory, and financial hurdles. "It took five years, but we won one hundred out of one hundred battles and raised capital in the midst of the global financial crisis," Yossi proudly recalls.

In 2011, Arava Power inaugurated Israel's and the Middle East's first solar field on Kibbutz Ketura. Proud but not yet satisfied, Yossi and his partners continued to expand the project. Thanks to his efforts and those of his partners, including the municipality, by 2020 the entire Arava region of Israel was powered by the sun during the day. By 2025 they are on track to power the entire Arava region both night and day. This unprecedented accomplishment earned Yossi the nickname Captain Sunshine, and for a few years he would sport a bright yellow kippah on his head wherever he went.

As always, Yossi had his eyes on the next plan. He dreamed of transforming Israel into a renewable light unto the nations.

Around the same time that Yossi launched Arava Power, an acquaintance named Anne Heyman founded a village in Rwanda called Agahozo-Shalom Youth Village (ASYV), for children orphaned in the aftermath of the 1994 genocide against the Tutsi. As youngsters in the 1970s, Yossi and Anne had both been a part of Young Judaea and had both volunteered on Kibbutz Ketura, albeit at different times.

There was a natural synergy. Anne was looking for ways to make ASYV more self-sustaining, and Yossi, who had launched an international arm of Arava Power called Gigawatt Global, was searching for the right project to demonstrate a quadruple-bottom-line approach to solar investments in Africa. He was certain he could generate healthy returns for investors, protect the environment, alleviate hardship, and enhance the reputation of Israel and the Jewish people. Anne was keen for

ASYV to be the pilot site, and by 2014 Gigawatt Global had built a vast solar field, where 28,360 solar panels are laid out in the shape of the continent of Africa on land leased from ASYV. It was the first utility-scale, grid-connected, commercial solar field in sub-Sahara Africa. When it went live, the solar field was supplying 6 percent of Rwanda's total power needs.

Today, Gigawatt Global is developing solar fields in ten African countries: Rwanda, South Sudan, Ethiopia, Kenya, Burundi, Mozambique, Nigeria, Liberia, Guinea, and Uganda. In 2023, Yossi cut the ribbon with the president of Burundi on a solar field that is supplying 10 percent of the country's needs. They are now exploring ten additional countries, many of which don't have formal ties to Israel. Naturally, Yossi isn't done. He sees Israel and Judaism as a platform for sourcing sustainable solutions to global challenges and takes inspiration from early Zionist intellectual Ahad Ha'am, who said, "Judaism…shall have as its focus point the ideal of our nation's unity and its free development through the expression of universal human values on the terms of its own distinctive spirit."

A living embodiment of Ahad Ha'am's vision, Yossi is on a mission to better the entire world, both inside Israel and out.

Yossi's Postscript

Unlike most Israelis and Jews, my heart was breaking not only for our losses in Israel during the war, but also for Palestinian children and parents in Gaza. Every time I called my solar partner in Gaza, I wasn't sure if she was alive to answer or if she would recount another tragedy in her extended family.

My Gaza solar journey began with a vision for the region knowing that the sun doesn't recognize borders. It shines on everyone and could provide clean and affordable energy to all.

For a decade we tried to advance various solar projects in the West Bank with Palestinian partners with limited success. But during a 2017 conference hosted by the Arava Institute, an impressive leader named Tahani Abu Daqqa made a compelling case for solar and water in Gaza. We joined forces with her, the Arava Institute, and a Palestinian NGO called Damour to provide solar-powered Watergens that harvest water in the air using solar energy to produce drinking water in Gaza municipalities and hospitals.

Quietly, we built the first solar field in Gaza east of Khan Yunis after receiving permission from the IDF and using private funding. We couldn't manage to secure funds from the international community as they prioritize diesel fuel or gas, giving into special interests that benefit Hamas rather than meet local needs.

For obvious reasons, our involvement in building the solar field was a secret. After it was mistakenly damaged during the war, Tahani bravely co-authored a Newsweek op-ed with me to outline our shared vision for solar and water in Gaza. We continue to seek grants and impact investments to scale our life-giving projects throughout Gaza.

PRAGMATISM

"We have been forced to find solutions to problems that large, wealthy, powerful states had never encountered."

—Golda Meir

Israel's founding on May 14, 1948, will stand in perpetuity as a transformative moment for the Jewish people. As miraculous as the occasion was, it didn't take long for a sober realization to take hold. There was a war to fight, refugees to feed and house, infrastructure to build, school systems to run, hospitals to operate, and an economy to jump-start. What choice was there but to confront each task head on? For three-quarters of a century, Israelis have been turning adversity into advantages through perseverance and simple pragmatism.

In Israel's formative years, tens of thousands of children orphaned by the Holocaust needed to be raised and cared for. The solution came in the form of youth villages set up throughout the country to educate and care for these children. One of these settlements, Yemin Orde Youth Village, has sat atop Mount Carmel in northern Israel since 1953 and is named in memory of British Major General Orde Charles Wingate. General Wingate arrived in pre-state Israel as an intelligence officer in 1936, when bands of Arab rioters were launching regular attacks on both the British and the Jews. Wingate, a brilliant tactician tasked with training Jewish fighters to repel these attacks, conceived the idea of "Special Night Squads," a Jewish fighting force that protected dozens of settlements during the Arab Revolt of 1936–1939. He trained iconic military leaders such as Yigal Allon and Moshe Dayan, who would later form the core of the Israel Defense Forces.

An enthusiastic Zionist, General Wingate learned Hebrew and dreamed of one day commanding the first modern Jewish army. He was an outspoken advocate for an independent Jewish state at a time when the British had largely backtracked on the Balfour Declaration, their promise to create a homeland for the Jews. Wingate urged Britain to "advance the foundation of an autonomous Jewish community with all the means in its power," adding ominously, "For pity's sake, let us do something just and honorable before it [world war] comes. Let us redeem our promises to Jewry and shame the devil of Nazism, Fascism and our own prejudices."[55]

A thorn in the side of the British, Wingate was transferred to Ethiopia and didn't survive to see the birth of the Jewish state he so believed in. That state would honor him, though, lending his name to Yemin Orde Youth Village and to streets throughout the country. Today, the youth village that bears his name in northern Israel is a sprawling community that serves as home and school to disadvantaged and at-risk youth. Removed from their homes to escape abuse, bullying, or violent neighborhoods, young people are provided with a home and family, personalized emotional and psychological support, and the chance to chart their own positive and productive futures.

---

[55] John Bierman and Colin Smith, *Fire in the Night: Wingate of Burma, Ethiopia, and Zion* (New York: Random House, 1999), 66.

"Death is nothing so long as one can survive through one's children."

—Rwandan proverb

Agahozo-Shalom Youth Village

Fifty years after its founding, the extraordinary success and reputation of Yemin Orde would inspire Jewish-American philanthropist Anne Heyman when she searched for a solution to help Rwanda's orphaned survivors of the genocide against the Tutsi. In 2005, Anne, a former Manhattan assistant district attorney, and her husband, Seth Merrin, sponsored an event at Tufts University about the genocide against the Tutsi. They listened intently to accounts of the horrors that had taken place in less than one hundred days in 1994, when an estimated one million Rwandans, mostly Tutsi, were butchered. Following the talk, Seth asked what the biggest problem facing Rwanda was, and the speaker answered that in a country with over one million orphans out of a population of eleven million people, there is no future.

"It popped out of my head: They should build youth villages," Anne told the *New York Times* in 2014.[56] "Israel had a solution to the orphan problem. Without a systematic solution, this is a problem that won't solve itself."

Anne couldn't shake the notion that there must be a way to help. She had never visited Rwanda, but conversations with various experts convinced her there was merit in the idea of

---

[56] Douglas Martin, "Anne Heyman, Who Rescued Rwandan Orphans, Dies at 52," *New York Times*, February 8, 2014, https://www.nytimes.com/2014/02/09/world/africa/anne-heyman-rwanda-rescuer-is-dead-at-52.html.

replicating the kibbutz-style youth villages established in Israel's early years. She envisioned a Rwandan-run youth village where the country's most vulnerable teenagers would have a safe, nurturing environment to obtain an education and receive support to recover from their trauma. She sent an email to the director of the Yemin Orde Youth Village. "You don't know me," the message began, "but I hope you might be able to help me in my mission." It was enough for then-director, Chaim Peri, to agree to help. He met with Anne, offered advice, and helped craft a model that could be emulated in Rwanda.

Anne, who was living in New York, traveled to Israel and Rwanda every couple of months, winning the support of the Rwandan government and recruiting a team of international experts. With each trip, a plan took shape. Anne and Seth raised over $12 million to purchase forty-four acres in a setting of lakes and hills in eastern Rwanda, an hour from Kigali. A beautiful complex of homes and school buildings was built atop a hill, Anne explained, "because children need to see far to go far." She chose the name Agahozo-Shalom Youth Village (ASYV). *Agahozo* is a Kinyarwanda word meaning "a place where tears are dried." *Shalom* is Hebrew for "peace."

ASYV opened its doors in 2008 to a stream of teenagers carrying paper bags containing all their possessions. Most had lost both of their parents; many had their entire families wiped out and no longer had a single living relative. Some did not even know their birthdays. Later, ASYV took in the children of parents who had died of AIDS. Other vulnerable children, including refugees from neighboring Burundi, were also accepted.

At ASYV, the well-being of the child drives decisions. Core beliefs dictate that exploring the past creates a healing bridge to the future and that individual well-being is the foundation for communal healing. Children deserve the best possible education. Beautiful surroundings and stable structures foster stability and wholeness. Indeed, ASYV is beautiful. Situated at the end of a red-dirt road set between rolling fields, the gate that welcomes visitors sports a hand-painted sign with the Kinyarwanda words "*Nureba kure, uzagera kure*" (If you see far, you will go far). Trees and flowering plants line the paths leading between the students' tidy modern homes and classrooms.

The emphasis at ASYV is on creating a stable family environment for each student. Teens live in homes, not dormitories. Each home has a Rwandan mother, referred to as Mama, who cares for around twenty students of the same gender. She makes sure they get to school on time and keep up with their homework and extracurricular activities, and she checks in with their teachers and therapists who help support their emotional and psychological needs. Most Mamas lost their own children in the genocide, and they view taking care of the ASYV teens as part personal healing and part civic duty. All teens start at ASYV with an enrichment year, a year focused on building community and ensuring everyone is on a similar academic footing.

With the school built and the staff in place, Anne needed to find a village director to realize her vision. The man she found was Jean-Claude Nkulikiyimfura, or JC, as the students fondly refer to him. JC's own story offers a lesson in inspiration to many ASYV students.

"I got my first passport when I was twenty-one years old," JC recounts. "Before that, I lived my life as a refugee." His parents, Silidion Nkulikiyimfura and Umulisa Xaverina, fled Rwanda as teenagers to escape the violence targeting Tutsi in the years before the 1994 genocide. They met, married, and had three boys, JC being the youngest.

Determined to build a good life for his sons and despite having only refugee papers, Silidion secured a job with the United Nations Development Program as an administrator in Bujumbura, Burundi. It was the start of a long and successful career as an international civil servant. As a boy JC lived in Mali, Ethiopia, Cameroon, Chad, Gambia, Burkina Faso, Sierra Leone, Niger, Senegal, Côte d'Ivoire, and Gabon. "We moved every two or three years, which was hard because it took us a year to adapt to a location and just as we started making friends and feeling comfortable, it was time to leave for the next posting," JC says. "But my parents were smart. Each time, they told us that the place we were going was the most incredible place. Mind you, some of these places didn't have electricity or clean water, but my parents found something to get us excited. They would say it has the most beautiful mountains or that we'd get to swim in the Atlantic Ocean. They always found something that would get three young boys excited."

JC's unusual childhood instilled resilience and optimism. No matter where they lived, his parents kept the family connected to its Rwandan roots by speaking Kinyarwanda at home and listening to traditional music. They told stories about Rwanda's physical beauty and the courage and integrity of Rwandan heroes who brought peace and stability to the region.

When JC started high school, his father was assigned to a new posting in Sierra Leone. In the past, JC's parents would find the local French international school to enroll their boys to allow for some continuity in their education. Sierra Leone, however, only had a primary French international school, and so JC was sent to a boarding school in the eastern part of France near the Swiss border. Afterward, he planned to follow in his older brother's footsteps to attend university in Montreal, Canada.

By the end of his high school years, JC's father was stationed in Niger, and JC joined him one day in a meeting with a woman from the US embassy. Making pleasantries, she asked JC about his plans for university. When he shared his intention to study in Canada, she scoffed and said, "Why would you pass over the United States to go to Canada? I have a much better idea, the University of Central Arkansas." Seeing JC's skepticism, she offered an angle she hoped would convince the teenage boy. "It's Scottie Pippen's alma mater," and then added, "It's just like UCLA, but without the L. Think of it as UCLA for poor people." Before he knew it, she had arranged for JC to take an English test at the embassy. A week later, he was admitted to the University of Central Arkansas, and before long JC arrived in the United States to attend college on a UN scholarship.

And so, JC found himself in Conway, Arkansas, population sixty-five thousand, some thirty miles north of Little Rock. With limited local opportunities to engage the outgoing young man, JC spent time balancing his studies and crisscrossing the United States, eventually visiting more than forty states. Because the freshman was interested in travel and writing, his father suggested his son study journalism. By his second year, he knew journalism wasn't the right fit. JC explains, "A journalist is supposed to be objective and impartial, but I have opinions. So, I switched over to PR where I felt more comfortable because I could advocate and share my point of view."

The end of the genocide in 1994 marked the beginning of a new era in Rwanda. Thousands of refugees were returning home, and JC wanted to be a part of the effort to rebuild Rwanda. He packed up his life in Arkansas and bought a one-way air ticket. When he landed in Kigali, he realized that he was no longer a refugee for the first time in his twenty-one years.

JC found work in the media office of the president of Rwanda, helping lawmakers develop an action plan to unite and rebuild the country. The goal was for the world to see Rwanda as an investment partner rather than just an aid recipient. Five years into the job, JC's father, the man who had guided and most inspired him, passed away. Heartbroken, JC honored his father's wish by returning to school to complete a graduate degree and then opened his own communications consultant firm, attracting major clients like the African Development Bank.

JC met Anne two years after ASYV opened its doors. She was looking for new board members, and JC's wife, Denise, had been suggested. Anne invited them to visit the village. As soon as they arrived, JC and Denise knew they were in a special place.

"I had imagined Anne to be a ninety-year-old woman who was trying to make up for a lifetime of sins by founding an orphanage," JC says. "I couldn't have been more wrong. Anne was young, vibrant, and easily the most charismatic and intelligent person I had ever met. I immediately knew I had met a visionary whose dreams were bigger than my wildest dreams."

They spent hours walking around ASYV and talking to Anne. Nothing came of the board position, but a year later a friend contacted JC to tell him that Anne was looking for someone to run the village. A one-hour chat between Anne and JC turned into hours of fervent planning, which eventually turned into a job offer. JC joined ASYV as village director in 2011. Together, they set about turning ASYV into a leading educational center and warm, vibrant community. They worked as partners, dreaming big dreams for the children of ASYV.

Anne sent JC to Israel to learn about Yemin Orde. In Israel, he was immersed in the ideas that still animate ASYV today. Anne's drive to establish ASYV was very much an expression of her commitment to her Jewishness. Students at ASYV, who are mostly Christian, speak casually about their commitment to tikkun olam—the Jewish values of serving one's community. Teenagers participate in initiatives such as raising funds for mosquito nets, teaching English at the local elementary school, or working with widows of the genocide. On the last Saturday of every month, the entire country takes part in government-mandated community service called "Umuganda," a Kinyarwanda word that means "coming together in common purpose to achieve an outcome."

Anne envisioned the village being truly self-sustaining. She wanted it to be able to meet the financial needs of its community and possibly even provide jobs for graduates. She reached out to Yossi Abramowitz—Captain Sunshine himself—who was by then one of three cofounders of the Arava Power Company, Gigawatt Global, pioneers of Israel's largest solar field. Anne invited the Abramowitz family to ASYV with a plan to convince Yossi to build a solar field for the school.

She told Yossi that the government was eager to increase the country's energy production, and she helped link Gigawatt Global to the Rwandan Energy Ministry. Solar fields require large tracts of land, and in Rwanda it's difficult to obtain huge plots of land because such acreage is by and large owned by private landowners. Anne had an advantage. When she bought the land for ASYV in 2007, she purchased tracts from ninety-six different families. School buildings took up about 20 percent of the land, and the rest had become dedicated farmland to enable ASYV to grow its own food. In Anne, Yossi found a fellow dreamer, and the two set to making the solar field a reality. Gigawatt Global leased land from ASYV and built 28,360 solar panels. From dawn till dusk, the computer-controlled photovoltaic panels tilt to track the sun from east to west. When the solar field opened in 2015, it produced 6 percent of Rwanda's energy.

Tragically, Anne didn't live to see the solar panels go online. She died at the age of fifty-two in a horse-riding accident shortly before the solar field opened. When news of her sudden death reached the village, Rwandan Youth Minister Jean P. Nsengimana wrote on Twitter that the village "just lost a mother." ASYV's announcement of Anne's death quoted a Rwandan proverb, "Death is nothing so long as one can survive through one's children." Today, a lush green garden surrounds a mango tree where Anne first signed the deed for the village's property. Her spirit is very much alive in the community. Hand-painted signs with her sayings are dotted around the property, and JC fondly shares memories and stories.

Thanks to Anne and her committed partners, ASYV has opened its doors to more than 1,700 young people. The village recruits from all thirty districts of Rwanda, searching out the country's most vulnerable teenagers. Each year, the school graduates around 125 students and boasts a 98 percent "pass" rate on Rwanda's national exam. Graduates have accepted scholarships to study abroad at such universities as Brown, British Columbia, and McGill. Most students return home afterward with dreams to contribute to building up Rwanda.

"It's amazing, once you help them heal, the greatness that can come out of a kid," JC exclaims. "We're not trying to create the next president of Rwanda. We're trying to create the next good citizen who cares for his or her family and community."

"If we can, we should."

—Dr. Ami Cohen

Save a Child's Heart

Israeli inspiration can be found in unexpected places all over the African continent, including in the medical field. This is in part thanks to the late Dr. Ami Cohen, an American-trained cardiac surgeon who made aliyah to Israel.

In 1995, while working as the head of pediatric cardiac surgery at the Wolfson Hospital in Holon, a suburb of Tel Aviv, Ami got a phone call from a pediatric cardiologist in Ethiopia who was looking for help treating two young patients with life-threatening conditions. Ethiopia, at the time, had no pediatric surgeons. Ami agreed to treat the two ill children and called in favors from his hospital colleagues. He found a team to help operate, and once they were discharged from hospital, he brought the children home to live with his own family throughout the long recuperation and until they were well enough to return home.

It wasn't long before Ami got another call asking for help operating on another child from a developing country, and then it was two more children, and then half a dozen more. Understanding the enormity of the need, he founded Save a Child's Heart to treat critically ill children suffering from heart disease in countries where access to pediatric heart care is limited or nonexistent.

The need was obvious. Each year, about 1.35 million babies are born with congenital heart disease. That's about one in every one hundred births. A quarter of these children need surgery to survive. If treated early enough, most can grow up to lead healthy lives, but it's estimated that 90 percent of these children live in regions without the necessary medical care, and so most of the children will die.

Ami's motto was straightforward: "If we can, we should." Save a Child's Heart sends medical teams to low-income countries to screen and treat children with cardiac diseases. They also bring children to Israel for specialized lifesaving surgeries. Ami understood that real transformation could only take place if countries could acquire the techniques and tools for themselves, so the organization places a huge emphasis on training. Each year, 150 medical team members from nearly twenty countries are brought to Israel for medical training programs that can last as long as six years.

Since 1995, Save a Child's Heart has operated on children from seventy countries and brought more than seven thousand children to Israel from low-income countries, including countries with whom Israel does not have diplomatic relations. About three hundred to four hundred children are treated every year. Half are Palestinians from the West Bank and Gaza and the Middle East, 45 percent are from African countries, and the rest come from all over the developing world.

Since the children must remain in Israel for two to three months after their operation for recuperation and observation, Save a Child's Heart built a home for them and their accompanying parents and nurses, as well as their trainee doctors from overseas. There are three key words spoken by all the house's multinational inhabitants: *kula* and *kulala* (Swahili for "eat" and "sleep"), as well as the Hebrew *balagan* ("mess").

Tragically, Ami didn't live to see how large and successful his organization would grow to become. Six years after its founding, he and his daughter were climbing Mount Kilimanjaro in Tanzania when Ami died suddenly from a combination of altitude sickness and heart problems. He was only forty-seven. The outpouring of grief was stunning. In addition to his many colleagues and patients in Israel, doctors from Nigeria and Ethiopia flew to Israel to pay their respects. A family from Gaza whose son was saved by Ami even attended the funeral.

In the aftermath of his death, it wasn't clear that Save a Child's Heart would continue. Ami had overseen every dimension of the work. He crafted the vision, traveled abroad on medical missions, made the arrangements for sick children to come to Israel, and raised the funds to keep the organization afloat. Three colleagues agreed to take the reins and keep the mission alive, and today they are aided by about one hundred doctors and nurses from Wolfson Hospital who volunteer their time and expertise.

Together, they have kept Ami's legacy alive by bringing life-saving care to more and more countries, including Zambia. The landlocked country in south-central Africa has a population of nearly twenty million people but until recently didn't have a single pediatric cardiac surgeon. A baby born in Zambia with severe cardiac disease had very few options unless the parents had the resources to take their baby abroad for care. For most families, it was financially impossible, and so their only chance was to hope that their child could get treatment from a visiting medical mission from overseas.

Save a Child's Heart knew that bringing pediatric cardiac expertise into Zambia would be transformative, and the first Zambian surgeon they trained was Dr. Mudaniso Kunani Ziwa. Ziwa has his own story of perseverance. The eldest of nine children born to two schoolteachers in a small provincial town in 1983, he was a sickly child. Growing up, he frequently contracted malaria and had to be hospitalized a few times each year. "Sitting sick in those hospitals, I hoped that someday I would be able to help people, like my doctors helped me. I set my goal early. In third grade, we learned about different professions, and of course I decided that I wanted to be a doctor. I grew up and held onto the dream of helping people who are suffering."

Earning a spot in medical school is a challenge anywhere, but particularly in Zambia. "People who want to become doctors or engineers or scientists all go to one school of natural sciences at the University of Zambia," Ziwa notes. "After a period, they are divided into streams depending on what they want to study, and then compete with other students to get picked for a program."

At the time, Zambia had just one medical school (today there are seven), and Ziwa's outstanding marks earned him an elusive spot in the program. He completed his medical training and specialized in general surgery, where he developed an interest in cardiac surgery. "There was no cardiac surgery program, but there were teams of doctors that arrived each year from Japan and Italy on medical missions," Ziwa says. "I would watch them in surgery. It thrilled me that they could stop a heart, fix a defect, close it back up, and then restart the heart."

Ziwa learned that Save a Child's Heart would visit Zambia's University Teaching Hospital, where he worked for its first-ever screening mission. As luck would have it, he was on duty to meet the team, and while showing them around the hospital, he conveyed his interest in training in pediatric cardiac surgery. Ziwa got his chance when the Zambian Ministry of Health signed a memorandum of understanding with Save a Child's Heart that included a promise to both treat children and train doctors. A team of medical professionals was chosen to train in Israel, including Ziwa who would train as a pediatric cardiac surgeon, while some of his colleagues would train in other specialties.

In 2018, Ziwa began his training in Israel, where he faced the ups and downs of living through conflicts and the COVID-19 pandemic. "Before I came, I heard stories from the media, mostly about tensions and fighting. But the reality is totally different. The people I've met are caring and kind, including when working with Palestinians. We see Palestinian patients on a daily basis, and everyone puts aside the news, and we treat each other as humankind."

Ziwa returned to Zambia in 2023 as the country's first pediatric cardiac surgeon. The transition into the country's health-care system was an adjustment. For starters, he had to adapt to working without the equipment available to him in Israel, but the National Heart Hospital in Lusaka is helping acquire specialized tools needed for pediatric cardiac surgery. For a period, he performed only straightforward cases, which gave him and the team time to learn how to coordinate with one another. He has since increased the complexity of cases with an eye toward sending fewer cases to Israel and enabling more patients to get treatment in Zambia.

"I dream that Zambia will be able to treat each and every pediatric cardiac case locally," Ziwa says. "The idea that a patient will die because we don't have the expertise or equipment should be a thing of the past. We should be able to take care of the cases in our country and even help operate on people from our neighboring countries."

Ziwa's Postscript

It's really sad what happened on October 7th and in the aftermath. However, this doesn't change my opinion about the people I met, both Israelis and Palestinians. They are loving and we worked well together. I really pray that all this will end, and that peace and harmony will be restored. It is always a pleasure to help the kids and to see them restored to health.

* * *

"You can't just talk. You need to do things."

—Russell Robinson

Jewish National Fund USA

In 1901, on the fourth day of the Fifth Zionist Congress in Basel, Switzerland, delegates spent the day considering an idea that had been on the agenda since the first congress four years earlier. At that time, a proposal had been made by Lithuanian-born rabbi and mathematics professor Zvi Hermann Schapira to establish a fund to purchase land in British-administered Palestine for the Jewish people everywhere. Five years later, and it seemed as if another year would pass without a commitment to act.

Theodor Herzl, who hadn't been present for much of the discussion, learned that delegates intended to table the motion yet again. He arrived to deliver an impassioned plea for the fund's immediate establishment. A vote was taken, and the motion passed by 105 to 82. They would call it the Jewish National Fund (Keren Kayemeth L'Israel in Hebrew) and set a goal of raising £200,000. A delegate immediately pledged the first donation, £10 in memory of Zvi Hermann Schapira, who had conceived of the idea but hadn't lived to see this moment. Theodor Herzl made the second donation and his aide, the third. In the spring of 1903, the fund purchased its first parcel of land, eight hundred acres in Hadera.

Over the next fifty years, the Jewish National Fund would purchase land throughout Palestine. Jews all over the world collected spare change in signature blue tin boxes. By the time Israel became a state in 1948, 233 of the 305 towns where Jews in the new state lived were on land bought by the JNF.[57] Since then, JNF has helped build the modern state of Israel by planting hundreds of millions of trees, building vital water reservoirs, developing infrastructure to help settle new immigrants, conserving scarce natural resources, and investing in cutting-edge research to transform desert lands into lush farms that can feed a growing population.

Almost 125 years after its founding, JNF retains its pioneering spirit. As CEO of Jewish National Fund USA, Russell Robinson explains, "JNF was pioneers in 1901 when they built the foundations for a Jewish state. They were pioneers in 1948 when they developed the institutions of the state." He goes on: "And we're still pioneering today. You can't just talk. You need to do things. We are transforming the Negev and Galilee to accommodate Israel's booming population. When you drive through the Negev Desert, you'll see lush farms growing figs, pomelos, peppers, and strawberries. In the future, when people ask about Israel and its neighbors, instead of asking who makes a better tank, we hope they'll ask who grows a better pomelo."

This dream is being realized by institutions like the Central Arava Research and Development Center, which is develop-

[57] Jewish National Fund USA, "Our History, 1901: It All Started with a Dream," https://www.jnf.org/our-history.

ing new crops and improving existing techniques so farmers in the Arava Valley can compete in the global produce market. Bordering the R&D Center is the Kasser Joint Institute for Food, Water, and Energy Security, a collaboration between Jewish National Fund, the University of Arizona, and the Arava Valley regional councils. The institute develops techniques and technologies to aid communities in arid and hyper-arid low-income countries in addressing their food, water, and energy insecurities cost-effectively and sustainably. Two other institutions supported by Jewish National Fund are also findings solutions for Israel and other arid countries—the Arava Institute for Environmental Studies and the Arava International Center for Agricultural Training.

"I believe in science as a catalyst to bring people together."

—Dr. Tareq Abu Hamed

Arava Institute for Environmental Studies

In a region known for conflict, few challenges are more daunting than navigating the national, ideological, religious, cultural, and political dynamics of the Israeli-Palestinian conflict. Tareq Abu Hamed is confronting these challenges head-on, certain that science can unlock solutions.

For many years, Tareq had a front-row seat to the hardships of conflict. Growing up in the village of Sur Baher, on the southeastern outskirts of East Jerusalem, he attended high school just outside the Old City of Jerusalem during the First Intifada of the late 1980s. Most days, he had to navigate checkpoints, and some days he found himself ordered to stand against a wall for hours on end. "There were also nights when IDF soldiers barged into our home," Tareq recounts. "They would wake us up at two o'clock in the morning to clean the stones from the streets and force us to erase graffiti from the walls. That was life."

When he was sixteen, Tareq worked in the cherry orchards of nearby Kibbutz Ramat Rachel. He learned English from volunteers and got his first glimpse of what it was like to operate in two different worlds. Worn down by the conflict, Tareq moved to Turkey after graduating high school to study chemical engineering and eventually completed both his master's and PhD degrees. The world of academia fed his curiosity and offered a more level playing field. He went on to complete two postdoctoral degrees, one at Israel's Weizmann Institute of Science and another at the University of Minnesota's Mechanical Engineering Department Solar Energy Lab.

While studying in Minnesota, Tareq was invited to apply for a position at the Arava Institute for Environmental Studies. Its mission appealed to him: to save the natural world by bringing people together. Founded in 1996, the institute runs academic programs, research centers, and international cooperation initiatives focusing on environmental challenges. Students from Israel and Jordan, along with Palestinians from the West Bank and the Gaza Strip, train together in the fields of sustainability and the environment. The institute is a unique oasis to bring people together and foster regional environmental leadership.

The Arava Institute is situated deep in Israel's Negev Desert on Kibbutz Ketura, where summer temperatures reach staggering heights. The hyper-arid region gets less than one inch of rainfall each year. The soil is chalky, dry, and salty. The average summer day is forty-plus degrees Celsius (one hundred and four degrees Fahrenheit), and at night the temperature drops only ten degrees. The harsh conditions meant that the region was mostly desolate until the 1950s, when a couple of idealistic pioneers decided to start a community. People thought they were crazy given the desert's brutal elements, but Ben-Gurion believed the Negev could be filled with vibrant communities. Experts were sent to test the soil and water, and most agreed that nothing would grow, except for one agronomist who said that if they found an efficient way to use water, maybe it could happen. Ben-Gurion was willing to take a chance and gave the two youngsters permission to try.

Despite the punishing and inhospitable weather, today more than 40 percent of Israel's crops are grown in the desert. According to data collected by the Tony Blair Institute for Global Change, Israel's tomato yield is 300 tons per hectare, compared with a global average of 50 tons per hectare. It also produces 262 tons of citrus fruit per hectare, compared with 243 tons in North America and 211 tons in Europe. All this requires water. Farmers drill up to 1.5 kilometers underground to reach water from five aquifers. Even then, the challenges continue. The groundwater is brackish and needs to be treated before it can be used to irrigate plants. Since the Arava isn't connected to the national water carrier, drinking water needs to be desalinated before being piped into homes. Farmers use a combination of low-tech solutions (water pipes, screens, plastic, netting) with high-tech, computer-controlled methods to keep plants cool by day and warm by night, and to ensure they get the right mix of humidity, soil chemicals, and water. Because Israel has such hot summers, Israeli farmers begin the planting season in June and grow throughout the winter. That gives them an edge over North American and European farmers who grow only during the summer months. Over the winter, Israeli farmers can export their produce all over the world.

Tareq visited the Arava Institute at Kibbutz Ketura for the first time in August 2008 to give a lecture as part of the interview process for a faculty position. "It was the height of summer, and the temperature was brutal," Tareq says. "When I stepped out of my car and felt the heat radiating around me, I thought there was no way I could work in this tiny place in the middle of an unforgiving desert. But they had invited me, and I wanted to be respectful, so I gave my lecture. The director was very clever because as soon as I was done, he asked me to meet with some students. It took just fifteen minutes with those students for me to know that I was going to accept the job."

What struck Tareq was that unless he asked their names, he couldn't immediately tell whether a student was Israeli, Palestinian, or Jordanian. "I found a place where science and environmentalism provide the common ground to create connections between people of different backgrounds. I was hooked."

Tareq and his family made the nearly three-hundred-kilometer move from East Jerusalem to establish and run the institute's Center for Renewable Energy and Energy Conservation. The building that houses the school used to be a large turkey coop. It has thick mud walls to help keep the interior cool and solar panels lining the roof. Steps away from the building are date trees sprouted from a two-thousand-year-old seed. An Israeli archeologist had discovered thousands of date seeds buried under rubble during his excavations of Masada. More date seeds were found in caves near the Dead Sea. They all sat in storage for over forty years until scientists at the Arava Institute figured out how to germinate the ancient seeds, then grew them into fruit-producing trees.

From the Arava Institute, Tareq joined Israel's Science Ministry, where he became the director of engineering research. It was sometime later that he learned that members of the security establishment had opposed his candidacy, but the chief scientist insisted on having Tareq simply because he was the best candidate. Reflecting on the setbacks and discrimination he's faced all his life, Tareq offers, "My philosophy is to do the best I can in every situation. And I have found that success follows."

Focusing on the task before him, Tareq gathered data to show the Ministry of Finance how Israel had slipped down the ranks of engineering progress since the 1990s. He made a compelling case to increase the departmental budget by tens of millions of shekels and, with new funding secured, made investments in technologies related to water, energy, computer engineering, and nanotechnologies. Tareq's principled outlook and work ethic saw him quickly move up the ranks of the ministry, becoming deputy chief scientist, and then acting chief scientist, which made him the highest-ranking Palestinian in the Israeli government.

Even so, Tareq still found himself caught between two worlds. He was living in East Jerusalem among Palestinians and working for the Israeli government. As a public servant, he represented the government, which often put him at odds with his neighbors. "They would call me a 'normalizer' or a 'collaborator,'" Tareq confides. "What people don't understand is that Palestinians will be here forever. And Israelis will be here forever. We must find a way to live together."

In government, he would still occasionally be regarded with suspicion. His position required a great deal of international travel to represent Israel in scientific conferences and meetings, and he was often stopped by security at the airport and subjected to extra scrutiny and delays. It was this aggravation that eventually spurred him to apply for Israeli citizenship. Even so, navigating the politics of his job grew too frustrating, and he decided to return to the Arava Institute in 2016.

Back at the institute he found an outlet for his twin passions of education and coexistence. "This job brings together all the things that I care about," Tareq continues. "I believe in science as a catalyst to bring people together. Nature knows no boundaries. Environmental threats don't recognize borders, and science offers a means to build trust and get people talking to one another to find solutions." The school has recruitment teams in Jordan, the West Bank, and the United States. Recently, students from Gaza learned about the program from social media, and a few applied. The Arava Institute secured student permits on their behalf. Today, there are two Gazan students studying in the program. It's their first time leaving Gaza.

For some students, the Arava Institute offers a space for open dialogue and expression that they haven't yet experienced in their lives. "This isn't a honeymoon program. Our students discuss everything, especially the hard things," explains Tareq, who became executive director in 2021. "They talk about the Naqba (the "catastrophe" of Israel's founding), about what it's like to live in a refugee camp, or what it's like to serve in the Israeli army. As you can imagine, the discussions get heated and there may be shouting or crying, but they can't run away. We're in the middle of the desert, and there isn't anywhere to go. And even after a bitter argument, they share the same dining hall, classrooms, and dorm rooms. So, they learn to talk and talk and talk. It's not easy. One day it will dawn on a Palestinian student that his Israeli classmate goes to army reserve duty and serves at checkpoints in the West Bank. And it will occur to the Israeli student that his Palestinian classmate comes from a family that supports terrorism.

"Everyone lives in the shadow of the conflict," Tareq continues. "Too often, it prevents people from coming together and from partnering. Everyone uses the conflict as an excuse to discriminate. What we have is a group of human beings who have been badly hurt—physically and psychologically—and they are trying to overcome the trauma and learn to reconcile."

The fact that the Israeli institute is headed by a Palestinian is helpful. It's easier for Palestinians to say that they're working with Tareq rather than with an Israeli university. The institute provides a platform to facilitate partnership and cooperation, particularly between Israelis and Palestinians. "We live so close together," Tareq says, "so it doesn't matter where the pollution starts. If it starts in Israel, it impacts Jordan and Gaza. If it starts in the West Bank, it will pollute the air here in Israel. The environment can't wait for a peace treaty."

One of the projects Tareq is most proud of is a clean water initiative for the people of Gaza. The strip is home to two million people, 75 percent of whom are under the age of thirty. Tareq points out, "People work for seven or eight shekels a day, and they have somewhere between eight to twelve hours of working electricity. Ninety-five percent of Gaza's drinking water supply is not fit to drink. Life is incredibly hard for them." He notes, "We helped facilitate the purchase and installation of Israeli-designed systems that extract potable water from the air using solar-generated electric power. Each system can produce eight hundred cubic meters of drinking water a year."

Tareq and his colleagues convinced Israeli authorities to send the water generators to Gaza. At the same time, they used their contacts in the Palestinian Authority to convince Hamas to accept the machines. In May 2021, as rockets were flying from Gaza toward Israel and the IDF was striking back at Hamas targets, Tareq was anxious to know if the systems were still working. The day after the hostilities ended, they were sent photos of people waiting in line to get water. Two days later, they received requests from five Gazan municipalities for additional systems.

Another project is situated in the West Bank, where many Palestinian villages are not connected to a sewer system. Instead, the homes use septic tanks that are not well insulated, meaning waste leaks into the aquafers that supply their drinking water. Scientists at the Arava Institute developed a wastewater treatment system for houses to treat sewage so it can be used to irrigate farmlands. They also facilitated the construction of a wastewater pipe from the Ramallah region to Palestinian farmers in the Jordan Valley.

Today, Tareq commutes between a home in East Jerusalem and a home in Kibbutz Ketura. Outside his office in the Negev Desert is a small experimental farm where research is being done on renewable energy and water purification.

"The environment can be a catalyst for war or a catalyst for cooperation," Tareq summarizes. "In our region, cooperation is essential because the current sources of water and energy won't be sufficient for everyone. There is no other way but to cooperate. We don't have the luxury of giving up. This is a long game, and we are planting seeds for the future of this region."

Tareq's Postscript

We are continuing our work despite the current conflict. The Arava Institute remains unwavering in our commitment to advance peace and sustainability through science diplomacy and cross-border environmental cooperation. We believe it is this approach that will allow us to rise above conflict and ultimately deliver a better future for the region and the world.

We have added more flexibility to our programs given the circumstances, but a cohort of students from Israel, Palestine, the US, and other countries in the Middle East continues to live and study at Kibbutz Ketura.

Our environmental projects remain operational as well. For example, three potable Watergen machines in Gaza, installed by the Arava Institute between 2019 and 2023, continue to provide clean drinking water for 2,000 people daily.

* * *

"There's money in the soil."

Kenarava

Eighty kilometers north of Tareq's office in the Central Arava is another agricultural training program. Instead of attracting young people from the region, this school is attracting young men and women from developing countries all over the world.

At the helm is Hanni Arnon, a woman who never dreamed she would run an agricultural school. Born and raised in

Jerusalem, Hanni moved to the Arava in 1986 so her husband could follow his dream of becoming a farmer. Hanni fell in love with the tight-knit community. Given the remoteness of the region and limited services, members of the farming communities rely heavily on one another.

In the early 1990s, Israel and Thailand signed a bilateral agreement that would create a special work permit for Thai workers to work on Israeli farms and receive agricultural training. Through the agreement, the Thai government saw an opportunity to bring Israeli agricultural expertise to Thailand, while Israeli farmers would benefit from having a reliable cadre of employees, rather than the idealistic tourists who arrive at their farms to work for a few months at a time. Recognizing that the Thai workers would benefit from some formal training and a supportive community, Hanni founded the Arava International Center for Agricultural Training (AICAT).

The first cohort in 1994 had twenty-five students from Thailand, who learned techniques in planting, pest management, irrigation, soil, and water management. They also learned about postharvest management, agribusiness, market analysis, and other critical skills that farmers need to run a thriving business. Successful farmers must be able to sell their produce, work with suppliers, address food standards, navigate government regulations, and adhere to local laws. Hanni recounts how, on a visit to the center, Thailand's ambassador to Israel said to her, "Make them tough like you. Show them how you make a desert flourish."

Hanni has been working to fulfill that mission ever since. Over the years, and with support from Jewish National Fund, the school expanded to take students from sixteen different countries in Africa, Asia, and the Pacific Islands. Today, twelve hundred young adults join the program each year. Many come from countries that, relative to Israel, have better weather, better soil, and more water, but the countries are nonetheless poor. At AICAT, students learn to run profitable farms by training them to be entrepreneurs. To make this possible, the school makes every effort to remove financial barriers to participation. Students are asked to pay for their flight to Israel, but if the costs are prohibitive, AICAT encourages them to take a loan to buy the ticket and guarantees the student will be able to repay the loan within three months. Students spend one day a week in the classroom and five days a week working alongside Israeli farmers on their farms. In this way, they earn enough money to pay tuition, cover their return airfare, and build some savings.

"The students arrive in Israel in August when the fields are empty," Hanni says. "They then grow alongside the plants over the course of ten months. They are learning through the growing season. In June, at the end of the agricultural season, the students graduate. Before going home, they can apply for a grant, funded by Jewish National Fund, to establish an agricultural business back home."

Students who attend AICAT must have already studied agriculture in their home country. Hanni and her team recruit through a network of overseas universities, including from countries that have no diplomatic relations with Israel.

One such student is Lia Simanjuntak, now age twenty-nine. Lia grew up in a small village on Indonesia's Seram Island. From the time she was six, she worked alongside her parents, brother, and sister on their small family farm. Depending on the season, her father would plant green beans, water spinach, cabbage, peanuts, eggplants, and other vegetables in rotation. They grew enough food to feed their family and had just a little left over to sell in the local village market.

In university, Lia studied agriculture and heard about AICAT from an older student who had attended the program. Curious, she tried to look up the school online, but she found that many Israeli websites were blocked by the Indonesian government, given that Jerusalem and Jakarta have no direct relations. The Israel-Palestinian conflict is an emotional issue in the world's most populous Muslim-majority nation, whose 277 million people have sided with the Palestinian cause since Israel's founding.

Lia kept searching and found YouTube videos made by AICAT students, as well as a Facebook page for the school. She sent an email to the school asking about the ten-month training program, and the information she received back impressed her. Still, she was worried what other Indonesians would say if they learned that she had studied in Israel. The decision weighed on her, but she figured she'd apply and see what happened.

When AICAT offered her a spot in their program, she knew it was a once-in-a-lifetime opportunity and accepted. She even turned down an offer to attend a program in the Netherlands so that she could study in Israel. The Israeli embassy in Singapore issued a visa and rather than stamping her passport, sent the visa attached to a slip of paper that she could keep separate from her passport. Flying to and from Israel via Thailand, she would be able to return to Indonesia without an immigration official seeing that she had been to Israel.

When Lia arrived at AICAT along with eighty-five other students from Indonesia, she was bursting with enthusiasm. "People will save money for years so they can take a trip to Israel, visit Biblical sites, and tour the country," she says. "I was going to get to live in Israel for ten months, see the holy sites, and learn about the culture." Most of all, she was excited to learn farming techniques from Israel. "The way they grow things in the Arava, you would think it's Europe. And you may think that in a Middle Eastern desert they would only grow dates. But Israel has figured out how to grow so many foods. It's a miracle."

The first time she saw bell peppers growing was particularly exciting. "I was speechless when I saw them. In Indonesia, we have peppers that are mostly spicy and not sweet. I had been waiting to see these Israeli peppers with my own eyes," she reports with enthusiasm. "I asked Uri, the farmer, if I could try them, and he told me to eat it like I'd eat an apple. I still remember the taste. I called my family and told them about this pepper that was totally delicious."

Lia soon found that, unlike at home, days on the farm were highly structured, with set working times and fixed breaks. Over the course of her months of study, she absorbed as much as she could from her teachers and took a special interest in the business of farming. She learned to assess the volume of produce to pick so that it would match market demands and then calculate the timing for picking and packing, taking into account transportation timing so that the goods would be high quality when they reached the consumer. She learned to manage software and machines that add stickers with barcodes to produce, and to adapt the codes for international markets where Israeli bell peppers are exported. Lia's passion for farming was so evident that AICAT asked her to return for a second year as a group leader, to help other students maximize their experience at the school.

Lia and Jose, another AICAT graduate from the same Indonesian village, were awarded a $6500 grant to start their own business. They plan to use a plot of land owned by Jose's family to start a nutmeg farm. Employing skills learned at AICAT, they are confident that they can improve the quality of production in the region, tap into a local and international market, and set up a demonstration farm to assist other farmers. At present, most farmers are only using the seeds of the nutmeg, but Lia and Jose also plan to collect the fruit to produce syrups and jams as a second business line. The grant will help them purchase a drip irrigation system, build a warehouse to store their harvest, buy equipment to make syrup, and market their new business. Lia also plans to help her father with his farm and make it more sustainable. On a trip home, she showed him how Israeli farmers remove the first fruits or buds from the crops, so the plants will conserve nutrients and yield better crops. That alone helped her father grow stronger crops.

By 2023, AICAT boasted twenty thousand graduates of its program. Three of them are Kenyans named Ronald Diang'a, Kenneth Chepkwony Kiplang'at, and Yvonne Kiere.

Ronald never planned on becoming a farmer. In fact, if you told him he would one day train a generation of young Kenyan farmers, he would have thought you crazy. His father, Ibrahim, was a self-starter who studied until his family couldn't afford his student fees. He switched to carpentry and found work in a Nairobi hotel. Ibrahim eventually saved up the money to open his own business and used the profits to buy parcels of land in Homa Bay, a town on the south shore of Lake Victoria in Western Kenya. He became a farmer, growing sugar cane and selling it to a nearby sugar factory. Ibrahim married three wives and fathered seventeen children, of whom Ronald is the youngest boy and second-youngest child. Remembering his own bitter disappointment at having to leave school, Ibrahim paid for all seventeen of his sons and daughters to attend university.

Ronald enrolled in the University of Nairobi to study geology. When he graduated in 2016, Israel and Kenya signed an agreement to send young Kenyans to AICAT. The National Irrigation Board offered Ronald one of these coveted placements.

"I'm a strong Christian," Ronald explains. "Israel is the land where every Christian wants to be, so I really wanted to go and see the places I had heard about and read about in the Bible." His excitement was mixed with trepidation. "I only knew Israel as a war-torn country. That's how I saw it on all the news broadcasts, and I was honestly afraid a missile would land on my head."

Summers in the Negev are long and punishing. "To be honest, I wanted to go home," Ronald confesses. "Between the heat and hard work, it was almost unbearable. But after three months, I saw that spending so much time on a farm was the best way to learn. We were immersed in growing crops and learning from experts. I have so much respect for those farmers. They wake up at five a.m. every day and go straight to their farm and get to work."

The more he learned, the more Ronald considered how he would bring everything he learned back to Kenya, where food insecurity is still widespread. Most young Kenyans living in rural areas dismiss the notion of farming as a livelihood because they see it as antiquated and unprofitable, particularly if they saw their parents struggle to make ends meet. They often migrate to large cities in search of opportunities, where they face an uncertain future. Ronald knew that with the right knowledge and tools, agriculture offered enormous opportunities. A vague idea took shape in his mind. There were so many Kenyans studying in the Arava program that perhaps they could work together to help farmers back home. He shared his idea with the other

Kenyan students and was disappointed to find that most weren't interested. A few students thought his idea had promise.

One was Kenneth.

For Kenneth, agriculture is deeply personal. He grew up in Nandi County, a lush green region on the western edge of Kenya's Great Rift Valley. Despite the abundance of rain in the region, as a boy he watched his father and many others struggle to earn a living from farming. Lots of families didn't have enough food. By the time Kenneth finished high school, his father had failed at crop farming and switched to keeping dairy cows.

Unlike many young Kenyans, who dismiss farming because of the hardships of their parents, Kenneth began to study agriculture so he could make things easier for his father.

"Many of the farmers are tied to the traditional way of farming, and it simply wasn't profitable," Kenneth explains. "In Nandi County, people grow maize. It's a staple of the local diet so everyone plants it, but then supply is too high, and prices drop. Farmers ignore current trends. They're not seeing that people want to diversify their diets to improve nutrition. Farmers need to make a series of choices before they plant anything, including studying the market to understand prices, assess demand, and source buyers."

Farmers in Kenya and other low-income countries face a range of challenges. First, traditional farming techniques are producing less than in the past. Kenneth elaborates: "Our parents were monocropping, meaning they were growing a single crop year after year on the same land, which damages the soil ecology by depleting or reducing the diversity of soil nutrients." There are also new advancements to consider. "Using indigenous seeds, it takes six months to grow maize. Introduce farmers to improved seeds, and their crops grow faster. This is important because people used to have much larger tracts of land, but with the population growing, land is being increasingly divided, so farmers need to grow more in less space."

He turns to the subject of rainfall. "Our grandparents used to follow the seasons and know the right time to plant and the right time to harvest. But in the last twenty years, the seasons have become less predictable, and rain is more erratic. Today, we can use technology for weather intelligence to help farmers get accurate localized weather data. Science has a big role to play in helping farmers. Shifting from reliance on seasonal rains, and adopting drip irrigation, for example, means farmers can farm more reliably year-round."

Still determined to help his father, Kenneth enrolled in the Animal Health Production and Processing program at Jomo Kenyatta University of Agriculture and Technology. In his third year, he learned about the opportunity for young Kenyans to get agricultural training in Israel. Setting aside his fears, Kenneth applied for an eleven-month work-study program at AICAT. He was thrilled to be accepted. The flight to Israel would be both his first time on a plane and his first-time leaving Kenya.

The Arava is a desert valley that extends from the Dead Sea in central Israel to Eilat in the south. The farms in the region become schoolrooms for AICAT students. Kenneth was one of 102 Kenyans in the program, joining over 1,000 other young people from Ethiopia, Laos, Cambodia, Myanmar, Thailand, and Vietnam. The school's motto is "learning by doing." Smiling, Kenneth describes what that means. "So, we spent five days a week on a farm getting practical training, and one day in the classroom studying theory. Saturday, we get Shabbat and a rest."

Kenneth was assigned to work with farmers at Kibbutz Lotan and spent his days in the kibbutz's date orchards. He learned that the kibbutz also had a dairy farm. Seeing a chance to learn his father's business, he convinced kibbutz leaders to let him also work part-time in the dairy. He was not pleased to learn that his shift would be from two o'clock to six o'clock in the morning each Saturday, when he and one other worker would be responsible for milking four hundred cows.

"Milking takes place three times a day," Kenneth says. "We follow the schedule of the cows, not the humans. For the cows, those are normal hours." When the milking was done, he'd get a couple hours of rest and then set off on his bicycle, the first purchase made with his first paycheck, and spend the day exploring the Arava Desert, taking photographs, and visiting students on other farms. That's how he met Ronald.

Kenneth loved Ronald's idea of bringing the knowledge and skills they had learned in Israel to Kenyan farmers. The two spent hours discussing ways they could make a real difference in Kenya. "When it came to finding a name for our project," Kenneth relates, "we knew we wanted to give credit to Israel. So, we came up with Kenarava by putting together Kenya and Arava." He pauses and then says with a laugh, "I promise the 'Ken' is for Kenya and not Kenneth."

Ronald and Kenneth completed their studies and returned to Kenya in 2017. Back home, they met with dozens of farmers to understand their needs. They still weren't clear on exactly what they would do, just that they wanted to find a way to help farmers. As Ronald explains, "We didn't have a clear plan. Things just took shape as we went along. But I knew we needed some expert guidance." Ronald turned to Caroline Kimetto, his brother's fiancée, a Harvard graduate who worked for a

Washington, DC–based consulting firm. Caroline suggested that Kenarava serve as an agricultural consultancy firm to advise and assist farmers.

In 2017, Ronald, Kenneth, and Yvonne Kiere, another AICAT graduate, formally founded Kenarava. In those early days, the three ran training sessions for farmers, who were impressed by their know-how. Word spread, and a local television station interviewed the three young entrepreneurs. That publicity helped attract more interest, but still the company was struggling to turn a profit. A friend suggested they promote themselves by hosting a dinner and positioning themselves as the youthful face of agriculture. Another friend suggested they adopt the tagline, "There's money in the soil."

Ronald, Kenneth, and Yvonne decided to take a chance and host a formal dinner at a local hotel. "We had no money in the bank, but we got lucky," Ronald says. "The hotel required payment up front but looked the other way and agreed to let us pay afterwards." The three entrepreneurs were gambling on selling enough tickets to cover their costs. Their first stroke of luck came when Noah Gendler, Israel's ambassador to Kenya at the time, agreed to provide funding for the event. The next stroke of luck was that he agreed to be the keynote speaker. Ronald recounts, "His attendance gave the event legitimacy. It attracted the attention of all the local newspapers, and suddenly everyone wanted to know who we were."

Dubbed the National Youth in Agriculture Forum, the dinner attracted 150 guests. Ronald, Kenneth, and Yvonne were able to settle their hotel bill, and even better, lots of companies suddenly wanted to partner with them. The dinner has since become a prominent annual event, attracting members of Kenya's government, UN officials, and leaders in the agribusiness sector. And of course, each year, the dinner is attended by the Israeli ambassador.

Today, Kenarava is a successful agricultural consulting business providing solutions to the challenges of food and environmental security. It offers agricultural advisory services to farmers, codesigns projects with corporations, runs training programs using model farms, and for a short while even exported pineapples grown by a Kenyan women's cooperative to Israel.

With every project, Ronald and his partners are proving to young Kenyans that there is indeed money in the soil and they can make a good living to support their families if they apply techniques like the ones used by Israeli farmers in arid environments. Kenarava helps farmers grow more and better crops, cope with water shortages, source high-quality seeds, mitigate against pests and postharvest losses, and connect with markets. Thanks to their training and network of relationships, they serve as the bridge between farmers and agricultural corporations, advising on communications and interventions.

Kenarava has earned major contracts including from UN Women in Ethiopia. Ronald has been awarded entrepreneur of the year and founder of the year honors, and listed as one of the top ten best social innovators.

Women and youth empowerment are front and center in their business model. Ronald is particularly proud that 90 percent of the guests at their annual dinners are women and youth. "We are young ourselves, and youth are the future of this country. If you look at international reports, you'll see that over 60 percent of the agricultural workforce is women. If you want to drive impact in agriculture, you absolutely must partner with women."

I joined Ronald and Yvonne on a farm in Thika, about one hour north of Nairobi. They introduced me to Peter, another AICAT graduate, who rented land from a local farmer. Peter is passionate about showing other young Kenyans that they can build sustainable futures in their own backyards by learning to farm more efficiently. Before studying in Israel, Peter relied on rainwater to irrigate his crops. Being weather-dependent added a lot of risk to farming. He has since introduced drip irrigation, a technique pioneered in Israel, which has provided stability and improved his crop yields.

On another visit to Kenya, Ronald and Kenneth introduced me to Zipporah at a farm near Kitengela, south of Nairobi. Zipporah, who prefers to be called Zippy, is an energetic thirty-something breaking boundaries for women and farming in Kenya. In her blue pleated blouse, black blazer, and striking necklace, she is also a fashion-forward farmer. Buzzing with excitement, she detailed the main hurdles she faced until she met Ronald at a conference in Kampala. She partnered with Kenarava to rent three acres of land and start her own farm. She walks us through the farm fields, past tidy rows of radishes, onions, and kale. She points out some of the technologies she has adopted and shares that her dream is to inspire other young women so that they too can earn a living and contribute to their household through farming. She invites skeptical young women to intern on her farm, teaching them both farming practices and the value of self-sustainability.

Since its founding, Kenarava has worked with thirty-five hundred Kenyan farmers, sharing Israeli agricultural expertise and helping boost productivity and profitability. Ronald, Kenneth, and Yvonne aim to train one hundred thousand farmers every year in the medium term and eventually impact a generation of Kenyan farmers.

"Israel is a desert. It rained only twice during my yearlong stay in the country," Kenneth says, "but Israeli farmers work the land all year round and remain profitable. We can bring that to Kenya."

Hanni's Postscript

On October 7, Hamas didn't distinguish between Israelis and the international students and foreign workers on the farms near Gaza. Blinded by hate, they murdered and abducted anyone they encountered. None of our students or alumni were directly impacted, but of course, they were deeply shaken. In the days that followed, AICAT alumni from all over the world reached out to see if we were ok and to offer messages of love and support.

Our newest cohort of students had arrived just a month before the attack. For two weeks we paused our program and reassured the students' parents that we would take care of them, even offering to bring the students into our own homes. By the end of October, AICAT restarted. Some countries, like Thailand and Fiji, sent their students home, but other countries, like Kenya, asked to send more students to Israel to demonstrate that they believed in our ability to keep the students safe and begin to rebuild. Over 100 students arrived at AICAT from Kenya just two months after the attack. Those of us who work in agriculture are a global community. Our students come to Israel to make a better life for themselves and their families. We will help them continue to do so.

Lia's Postscript

"This is a terrible tragedy not only for Israel, but for all humanity. At a time when we need peace and equality, the October 7 massacre has crushed me. I believe the basis of humanity is to live and create. I hope that eternal peace will be established, and people will live a prosperous life. I pray that all the hostages will come home safe and sound."

ADVENTURISM

"Everybody can acquire knowledge, and Israel is a country prepared to share its expertise with nations of the world."

—Shimon Peres

A big trip overseas has long been a rite of passage for young Israelis after they complete their military or national service. According to ISRAEL-Is, an Israeli NGO, 410,000 Israelis between the ages of twenty and twenty-four travel abroad each year, most of whom are discharged soldiers. After years of carrying the weight of securing their nation on their shoulders, travel feels both easy and liberating. Free from the strict, regimented routine of army life, travel offers the chance to unwind and recalibrate before starting a degree or a career.

Yonatan Bram was twenty-one years old when he finished his mandatory military service in 2004. The previous three years were a dull haze of exhausting training drills and the monotony of sitting in readiness in case his unit was activated. He had served in the prestigious Oketz Unit (*oketz* is Hebrew for "sting"), an infantry unit for dog handlers, assigned to securing Israel's northern border from terror infiltrations. His unit was situated just twenty kilometers from where his parents lived, which added a sense of gravity. Unlike friends who served in Jenin, Tulkarm, or other hotbeds of terrorist activity in the West Bank, Yonatan's time in the north was quiet. "I spent a lot of my service worried for my friends," he says. "I also spent a lot of time waiting around and just being really bored." Often, he would pass the time daydreaming about the big trip he would take after the army.

Twenty days following his discharge, Yonatan was on a plane with an open-ended ticket to Mexico. He had no fixed return date and no firm plans. On his first day abroad, he found his way to a bus station and thumbed through a *Lonely Planet* guide puzzling out how to get to Oaxaca. He would spend the next year trekking through Central and South America, interspersed with a trip to the United States, where he worked as a handyman and drove a Blue Bunny ice cream truck, to earn enough money to carry him through another few months of trekking.

Most of the time Yonatan traveled solo, but occasionally he'd join groups of other backpackers. "I made friends with Canadians, Germans, Danes, and Israelis," he recalls. "I was looking for fun, looking to decompress, looking to meet women, looking to party. I was reading romantic poems, journaling semi-profound thoughts, and offering rambling self-reflections. Most of the time, I was contemplating life."

Yonatan moved around a lot, sleeping in different hostels, or taking his backpack into the wilderness, walking all day, and tying a hammock between two trees when it grew dark. Sometimes, he'd consult a map, point at a destination, and start walking. Usually there was no path, and so he'd use the navigation skills he learned in the army to devise a route.

"It never crossed my mind to be afraid on those treks. I was young, and army life had taught me to be self-sufficient and fearless. I had a hunger for adventure, and I was constantly chasing fun. I remember making my way to a remote village high atop the mountains and feeling delighted to find that, even in that isolated place, I could buy a cold Fanta. There were lots of long, dusty rides on public buses or in the back of pickup trucks bouncing around. It was too bumpy to read and too loud to listen to music."

When the year was up, Yonatan was out of money but full of stories and a sense of self-reliance. "I had figured out how to adapt and knew I could work anything out. You can toss me anywhere and I'll get by, and I'm proud of myself for that."

Back home in Israel, he followed the course of many young Israelis, earning a degree, trying out different careers, and eventually getting married. Yonatan and his wife, Gili, decided to take a honeymoon year in Nepal working in rural communities, after Gili was offered a position with an Israeli nonprofit called Tevel b'Tzedek. They figured the time abroad and the unique experience would solidify their marriage. Both think back on that year with a lot of fondness for Nepal and its people. The more Yonatan learned about the country and the more time he spent partnering with locals, the more he thought about the ethics of traveling and working in developing countries.

"When I had traveled through Central and South America, I was not very politically aware. I didn't think about my privilege, or about class and economic differences from a critical perspective. I was just enjoying how far I could stretch ten shekels. There was a lot I had to learn."

Committed to the work, he started a master's program to study the ethical dilemmas faced by international development practitioners and eventually took the helm of Tevel b'Tzedek from its founder, Micha Odenheimer.

"I envisioned a sort of Jewish Peace Corps to connect Jews to the developing world and build a community of activists who can change the world."

—Micha Odenheimer

Tevel b'Tzedek

"You can't be global in every sense except ethics," Micha Odenheimer insists. "Israel's prosperity and power come with the obligation to look beyond ourselves and serve others." That sentiment led the American-born orthodox rabbi, journalist, and social activist to launch a successful initiative to combat poverty in rural Nepal and afterwards in Haiti, Burundi, and Zambia.

When Micha was growing up, justice was a central theme in the Odenheimer family. Born in Berkeley, California, thirteen years after the Holocaust to a refugee father from Nazi Germany, the shadow of World War II colored Micha's formative years. When he was twelve, the family spent two and a half months in Israel, and Micha became interested in religion. As he grew older, he struggled to find his religious footing, while navigating his growing disillusionment with Western culture. He enrolled in literature at Yale and later switched his major to religion so he could spend his Junior year studying at Hebrew University in Jerusalem.

By the time he graduated, he found his religious footing, and as a young rabbinical student in New York, Micha gravitated to the circle around the late Hasidic teacher and singer Rabbi Shlomo Carlebach. His synagogue on Manhattan's Upper West Side was focused on social justice, even serving as a drop-in center for the neighborhood's homeless population. When Shlomo would travel to Israel, he left Micha in charge of the synagogue, providing him with money, the names of homeless people, and instructions for how much each one should receive.

In 1988, Micha relocated to Israel with his wife. "Israel is the place where the future of the Jewish people is being determined; I wanted to be part of it," Micha has said. Having always been interested in writing, he took on freelance journalism projects. He was particularly interested in the story of the Ethiopian Jews who had immigrated to Israel in the early 1980s.

By the time Micha arrived in Israel, thousands of Ethiopian Jews from rural mountainous villages had made their way to Addis Ababa, waiting their chance to be flown to Israel. Sensing the chance to tell an important modern-day Exodus story, Micha bought an air ticket with his own money and set off. It didn't take long for him to fall in love with the country, its people, and the Jews of Ethiopia. "People had nothing, but they preserved tradition and community, the sustenance of what it means to be human," Micha recalls. The Jews he met also captured his heart. "They were poor, black, rural, illiterate—defying the conventional Western notion of Jewishness. They stretched our boundaries of Jewish identity."

It wasn't possible to get a journalist visa, so Micha kept a low profile while writing and filing stories in Israeli and American Jewish newspapers. Despite his best efforts, his writing drew a lot of attention, so much so that he got a call from the office of Mengistu Haile Mariam. "My first thought was that I'd be jailed or barred from the country," Micha recounts. "But instead it was an offer to interview the president. And the interview lasted three hours—and made waves in the international press."

In May 1991 Micha returned to Ethiopia on his fourth trip that year. By then, the country was torn by civil war, and rebels were closing in on the capital. Fearing for the well-being of the Jewish community that had gathered in Addis Ababa, the Israeli government launched Operation Solomon to bring them to Israel. Over the course of thirty-six hours, over fourteen thousand Ethiopian Jews were flown to Israel. As the last rescue plane was readying to leave, Micha had to decide whether to join the flight or stay behind and report on the fall of the regime. He stayed and spent a month in the chaotic capital, dodging danger.

Back in Israel, he was frustrated to see that not enough was being done to help the new Ethiopian immigrants resettle. He reported on the problems, making a point to note that the state was repeating the mistakes that had been made with Jewish immigrants from Arab countries in the 1950s. Micha saw a paternalistic system that ignored the cultural strengths of the Ethiopian Jews. Young Ethiopians were being directed into trade tracks, effectively denying them an academic education that would lead to greater social mobility. Angry at the injustice and determined to do more, Micha helped founded the Israel Association for Ethiopian Jews (IAEJ) to act as the community's lobby. In the coming years, the IAEJ repeatedly pressured the government, lobbying and using the Israeli and international press, demanding greater equality in housing and employment issues. It ultimately succeeded in reversing the Education Ministry's policy on trade schools and opening an academic track for young Ethiopian Israelis to complete college. Five years after founding IAEJ, Micha turned the organization over to emerging Ethiopian leaders, fulfilling his goal of the organization being led by and for the Ethiopian community. Just as he had more time on his hands, Micha got a call from a young Israeli who had been backpacking around Ethiopia and claimed to have found the last Jews of Ethiopia. Intrigued, he wanted to see for himself. So in 1998, Micha, along with a young Israeli and an Ethiopian doctor, set out for Quara, on the Sudanese border. The region was remote and largely inaccessible. "You go to Gondar and take a right for five hundred kilometers," Micha recounts. "It was so inaccessible that we couldn't take jeeps. We needed tractors."

Sure enough, they discovered a community of two thousand Jews. A feud between the Jews of Upper Quara and Lower Quara some years earlier had caused a rift that fractured the communities. Micha returned to Israel and led a campaign to convince the government that there were in fact Jews still in Ethiopia. A year later, the last Jews of Quara were airlifted to Israel.

Micha's restlessness led him to report from some of the most dangerous places on the planet. He went to Somalia during the famine, to Myanmar during martial law, to Iraq just after the Second Gulf War, to Bangladesh to report on intellectuals fighting the country's boycott against Israel, and to Nepal to interview Maoist rebels fighting the government.

Nepal, out of all of them, particularly enchanted him. The beautiful landscape, the simplicity and joy of its people, and their open affection for Israel. In 2005, Micha brought his family to India for a family vacation, and as they traversed the country, they met many young Israeli backpackers recently out of the army. He noticed that they generally spent time with other Israelis and had little interaction with Indians who were not in the tourist industry. "They were traveling through the East not only because it was cheap but because they wanted to understand the world," explains Micha. "I felt that many of them would want an opportunity to deepen their experience."

The trip sparked an idea. Micha knew these young Israelis had so much to give. "They are hardworking. They're used to improvising from the army and from living under threat. They have an amazing ability to connect. They're Western and not Western at the same time."

Many of these young people were keenly aware of the poverty in South Asia and wanted to help in some way, but there was no framework for them to do so. Micha realized he could serve as the bridge. "I wanted to influence a generation of young Israelis. I envisioned a sort of Jewish Peace Corps to connect Jews to the developing world and build a community of activists who can change the world."

In true Israeli form, Micha forged ahead before working out all the details. He raised funds and recruited his first cohort of sixteen young Israelis, figuring he could work out exactly what they would do later. He decided to begin the work in Nepal, which was easier to navigate bureaucratically than India and was considered the poorest country in Asia. Five weeks before the program was to begin, Micha flew to Kathmandu and arranged for his volunteers to work as interns in local NGOs. Some worked with street children, others with trafficked women, and still others in the local slums.

The program was a success, and in 2007, Micha formalized his volunteer program into an organization that he named Tevel b'Tzedek, inspired by a line from a psalm that means "the world with righteousness."

"Judaism," Micha explains, "is not only about going inward for our own history, but also about creating a more just, compassionate, and beautiful world. The highest level of charity is to help someone become self-sufficient, and that's how Tevel works." He continues, "We have to create a world where every human enjoys basic rights."

In time, makeshift arrangements were replaced with a systematic plan for tackling poverty. Each year, thousands of Nepalese migrated to cities looking for work, relinquishing their land and settling into overcrowded slums. Many ended up in Nepal's brick factories, which are infamous for their poor working conditions and polluted environment.

"We want to find a way for villagers to stay connected to their land, while being able to feed and support their families. That's becoming harder as the population has grown and deforestation has eroded farmland," says Micha. "Our goal is to make the villages places of opportunity. We help Nepali villagers increase their productivity so they can retain their farms and support their families."

Tevel brings Israeli teams of experts in agriculture, water conservation, education, and women's empowerment to train local Nepalese farmers. They learn agricultural skills that enable them to produce enough food to feed themselves and remain on their and in their communities. On the ground, operations were overseen by Bishnu Chapagain, a Nepali who joined a MASHAV training program and went on to complete a PhD in agronomy from Ben-Gurion University of the Negev. His agricultural training is critical to the organization's long-term project to introduce Nepali farmers to Israeli farming practices.

Tevel recruited both young Israeli volunteers and young Nepali volunteers to work together in the villages. Volunteers were given language and cultural lessons, then paired with local families to experience firsthand the conditions for rural families.

In 2019, I had the chance to see this work firsthand. On the appointed morning, I exited my Kathmandu hotel with a small group that I was leading to find a lineup of jeeps waiting to transport us. Our little bus was not equipped to safely traverse the winding, rock-pitted countryside roads. We set off for the town of Bethanchok, east of Kathmandu. Outside the city, we wound through farmlands and rice fields and bounced along mountain switchbacks and countryside roads.

We arrived midmorning and were greeted by Bishnu. The little street where we parked was crowded with small shops. Bishnu led us to a small tea kiosk and chatted with the vendor who ladled the steaming liquid into little paper cups for us. Sipping hot tea, we surveyed the scene. The street was lined with two-story buildings in pinks, yellows, and deep reds. Many shops had a long chain of marigolds hanging just below their signs. On the upper level were homes with colorful laundry drying on lines hung from their balconies. Narrow dirt streets were crowded with cars, motorcycles, and pedestrians. Stores had stacks of grain bags piled outside or metal canisters lining the walkways. School children in their tidy blue uniforms waved as they walked by on their way to or from school.

When everyone finished their tea, Bishnu explained that Tevel's work in Bethanchok focuses on helping locals increase their income through agricultural and tourism projects. They support agricultural training for local farmers and market facilitation to help with the sale of crops. At the same time, they developed a homestay program in which local villagers rent a room in their home to tourists and development volunteers who want to live and work in the surrounding area. Tevel's mission is to both empower community members and mobilize Nepali and international volunteers. The remoteness of the villages meant that volunteers must hike the mountains to get around;

share unheated cabins, outdoor squat toilets and showers; and carry water from village taps since there is no running water.

Bishnu led us by foot on a path through the rural mountain community. As we walked, Bishnu chatted about Tevel's focus on women and youth empowerment and promised we would meet with the locals who benefited from these programs later in the day. Seemingly inexhaustible, Bishnu scaled a series of hills, never losing his breath as we puffed and panted behind him. We finally reached the top, where a group of children gathered and shouted to us, "Namaste. Shalom. Hello."

About twenty-five local women greeted us with huge smiles and draped handmade marigold necklaces around our necks. We sat down together for a far-reaching conversation in which we learned about their lives and they learned about ours. Later that night, as my group sat together around a fire pit after dinner, our conversation kept returning to the conversation with those women. We were amazed by their confidence and courage to speak out against the injustices they have faced and the way they leaned on one another for support. Tevel has helped strengthen and empower their community. After the devastating Nepali earthquake in 2015, Tevel created a Youth Service Program, enrolling young adults from the villages in a two-year program in which they were trained to catalyze the entire village to engage in new modes of livelihood and community organization.

The youth-centered method—recalling the young pioneers of the kibbutz movement a century ago—proved effective. Over the past decade, Tevel has trained more than 50,000 rural farmers, 70 percent of whom are women. This has generated hundreds of thousands of dollars in new income annually for poor and marginalized rural villagers. Tevel has succeeded in transforming villages that were unable to grow enough food to feed themselves, to suppliers of thousands of tons of food annually to local markets. That success led them to expand their work around the globe, and they have brought over fifteen hundred Israeli and Jewish young people to volunteer in Nepal, Zambia, Haiti, and Burundi. "We take a long-term, comprehensive approach to village development. Many organizations focus on one thing: bringing drinking water or teaching agricultural skills. We look at the whole system of skills, resources, community institutions and infrastructure that are needed to change the economy from subsistence to small-scale commercial agriculture, including crops, poultry, and aquaculture."

Currently, Tevel's main project is in Zambia, where the organization is working in a village area called Mphande with five thousand residents. Currently the main source of income is from cutting down trees and burning them for charcoal, but the trees are dwindling and there is a danger of desertification. Tevel's comprehensive and youth-led approach—twenty-seven young adults from the village are enrolled in Tevel's two-year full-time Youth Service Program—aims to transform Mphande's livelihood within a five-year period.

With all of that under his belt, Micha isn't nearly ready to take a break. His devotion to social activism and Torah won't let him, not so long as there is work to be done to make this a more just, compassionate, and beautiful world.

"We as Israelis understand chaos and know how to deal with it."

—Yotam Polizer

IsraAID

Tevel b'Tzedek's most famous alumnus is probably Yotam Polizer.

Like Micha, Yotam has built a life around community service. He grew up in Harashim, a small village in Israel's northern Galilea. His parents, a social worker and school counselor, had four children—the youngest of whom, Ofer, was born with cerebral palsy. As a teenager, Yotam volunteered at Ofer's camp and later at a boarding school for children from underprivileged backgrounds. During his army service, his unit was assigned to run educational projects in communities around Gaza. The region is dotted with Bedouin communities, and Yotam was curious to learn more about their way of life. He took it upon himself to design a leadership program for Bedouin teens, which became so successful it was recognized for two years running in Israel's national Independence Day Ceremony. "The success," Yotam claims, "came from building trust with the local community. I learned that you need to come with a lot of humility and by showing real interest in people's lives and their culture."

Following his army service, Yotam did what thousands of other Israelis do—he saved up as much as he could and set off for his big trip in 2007. Unlike other young Israelis who followed the Hummus Trail in India, Yotam preferred to be off the beaten path, spending time in remote communities, talking to locals and learning their culture. A natural gift for languages, combined with sheer determination, saw him learn local dialects so that he could speak directly with locals.

A few months later, he joined a friend, and they crossed into neighboring Nepal to hike in the Himalayan mountains. Afterward, they made their way to Kathmandu, where a poster at the local Chabad House caught Yotam's eye. He says, "I saw a small ad for an organization which had been established to bring together Israeli Jewish backpackers to do volunteer work." It was an invitation for Israeli backpackers to join an evening program on social responsibility led by Tevel b'Tzedek. Yotam's interest was piqued, and he went to meet Micha and a group of Jewish and Israeli volunteers. The idea of volunteering in rural communities sounded exciting to him, and he decided to join for a few hours a week. Those few hours turned into three and a half years.

For the first few months, he learned Nepalese and worked with street children. Noting how adept he was with both speaking the language and working with locals, Micha offered Yotam a job working for Tevel b'Tzedek. Yotam also took a job with the Israeli embassy in Kathmandu, where he helped coordinate rescues for the twenty to thirty Israelis who run into trouble while hiking in the Himalayas each year. Since he was the only one who spoke fluent Nepalese, he was also assigned to interview migrant workers who applied for work visas, most of whom sought to become caregivers in Israel. It didn't take long for Yotam to identify and root out corruption on the part of agencies that were charging crippling rates to impoverished migrants. He compiled a dossier on the worst offenders and passed them to Israel's Ministry of Labor to launch a formal investigation.

Yotam returned to Israel in early 2011. A few weeks later, Japan was stuck by the strongest earthquake in its recorded history. The quake was powerful enough to shorten the Earth's day by throwing an extra wobble into its rotation. In less than an hour, the first of many tsunamis overcame the country's northern shores. Waves over 130 feet high killed 15,500 people, left 450,000 homeless, and crippled the infrastructure of the country. Eleven nuclear reactors at four power plants automatically shut down when they detected the earthquake's vibrations. But nuclear fuel requires cooling even when a plant is stopped. The Fukushima Daiichi plant had planned to use emergency diesel generators to continually pump cooling water to these reactors. Within an hour, the flooded generators failed. A hydrogen explosion tore through one of the reactors, releasing radiation.

Shachar Zahavi, one of the founders of IsraAID—an informal coalition of small NGOs providing assistance following earthquakes, hurricanes, and pandemics in humanitarian crises all across the world—reached out to Yotam. Shachar was about to send a team of Israeli doctors to Japan, and he asked Yotam to lead the delegation. Yotam had never been to Japan, didn't speak Japanese, and wasn't a medical professional; but after years in Nepal, he knew how to integrate with local communities, build partnerships, and manage complex logistics.

The flight to Tokyo was almost completely empty, as most everyone else was running away from the radiation. When Yotam and the team arrived, it became clear that a medical team wasn't what was needed because, tragically, there weren't a lot of survivors. After a month of assessing the needs of local communities, Yotam offered to run an art therapy program at a kindergarten in a town called Yamamoto-cho, where eight children and a teacher had been killed by the tsunami. The parents and teachers were surprised to see the children immerse themselves in the program and express their feelings for the first time since the devastation.

As Yotam makes clear, "The Japanese didn't really need support in terms of infrastructure or supplies. What they didn't have was emotional support. In Israel, because of our own traumas from conflict and the Holocaust, we have developed expertise in building community resilience and social support. So, we started to bring this knowledge to Japan."

From that first kindergarten, Yotam and the team expanded across town and eventually to ten cities across Japan, training three thousand social workers. Along the way, he was formally hired by IsraAID as its second employee and its country director in Japan. He stayed for over three years, became fluent in Japanese, and was introduced by the American ambassador in Japan to the woman who would later become his wife.

In time, he expanded IsraAID's projects beyond Japan. They worked with North Korean refugees in South Korea. In South Sudan they trained the first generation of social workers in the country, to provide support for victims of gender-based violence, such as sexual abuse and rape. In the Philippines, they started a trauma care program for survivors of the 2013 typhoon. In 2014, they deployed to Sierra Leone during the Ebola crisis.

On April 25, 2015, shortly before noon, a 7.8 magnitude earthquake struck central Nepal. The massive quake was felt as far as northern India and northwestern Bangladesh. It was the deadliest earthquake in the seismically active region in eighty-one years. Nearly nine thousand people died, and over twenty-two thousand suffered injuries. More than six hundred thousand structures in Kathmandu and other nearby towns were damaged or destroyed. The quake was followed by hundreds of aftershocks, and just seventeen days later, there was another major quake, registering 7.3 on the Richter scale. When all was said and done, over eight million people, about a third of the national population, were affected.

At the time, Yotam, who was IsraAID's South Asia regional manager, was in Japan. He booked a flight to Nepal to meet his team. "The chaos was evident upon landing," he recalled. "The airport was hectic and packed with a frenzy of people trying to leave Nepal, and others, like myself, trying to get in. A surreal mix of tourists desperate to exit and aid workers desperate to enter."

He checked in with local officials, international organizations, and the IDF delegation in Nepal, which had deployed search-and-rescue teams trained to locate survivors in the rubble of collapsed buildings. They also set up a field hospital, equipped with operating and intensive-care rooms, to provide medical services for the local population. Yotam and his team set out for one of the worst affected areas of Kathmandu. "The air was thick with dust, the roads full of rubble," he recollects. "Around me were devastating scenes of flattened homes, toppled temples, and collapsed buildings."

The team spent days searching for survivors. Five days after the earthquake, they were digging through rubble in Gongabu. They had already pulled out twenty-one dead bodies. Suddenly, someone told everyone to be quiet, because he thought he could hear someone calling for help. Yotam crawled inside a crevasse in the rubble and yelled out in Nepalese. From somewhere below him, he heard someone whisper the word "*duktsha*," which means "it hurts." IsraAID led a ten-hour rescue effort by teams from France, Norway, and Nepal to reach Krishna Devi Khadka, a twenty-four-year-old housekeeper trapped in the rubble of the hotel where she worked. She was evacuated to the IDF field hospital and miraculously survived the ordeal. The story was all over the news.

Two years later, Yotam was appointed the co-CEO of IsraAID, together with his friend, Voni Glick. Together, they grew the organization, opened an office in Tel Aviv, formalized operations around the world, led major fundraising campaigns, hired a staff of over three hundred people across fourteen countries, with around 70 percent of its employees being local to the nations where they work. In its twenty years of operations, IsraAID has worked in sixty-four countries. Under Yotam's leadership, IsraAID has become Israel's leading humanitarian aid agency, bringing rapid, effective help to desperate people and staying on the ground to assist with the long-term impacts of disasters.

"In many different crises and contexts, we learned what we're good at and what added value Israel, as a country, has to offer," Yotam says, "because we're not operating in a vacuum. There are other organizations. You have the Red Cross, you have the UN, and they have billions of dollars at their disposal. We're a small organization representing a small country. So what do we have to offer? Israel has by necessity become an expert in several areas, and IsraAID has harnessed that expertise and best practices to assist the world's most vulnerable communities in disaster areas all over the world."

IsraAID's core areas of support are public health, psychosocial support, clean water and sanitation, and education. "Whether it's water technology that was developed here because of water scarcity, or whether it's trauma counseling and prevention of post-trauma stress because of our own traumas, we have both expertise and a culture of improvisation," Yotam adds. "We as Israelis thrive in chaos. When things are too organized or bureaucratic, we can't manage. So, we go to a disaster area in the most remote parts of the world, and it's very chaotic. That's fine. We understand chaos and know how to deal with it. We also know how to find quick solutions."

IsraAID's relatively small size has proven to be an advantage, as it allows the organization to be flexible and dynamic. In every country, they seek out a local partner, be it a church or mosque, or the local Jewish committee, or local government, or whoever might help them fulfill their mission. In many ways, IsraAID is the essence of the best of Israel—it's small, adaptable, and innovative. It thrives in situations of chaos and can find solutions for seemingly impossible situations.

"That's our goal—to bridge gaps," Yotam continues. "When disaster strikes, we usually arrive within the first seventy-two hours. But to be honest, there are lots of organizations that arrive quickly. The difference is that we stay long after everyone else has left. Most organizations go for a few weeks or months. But after three months, they are gone. Why? Because, unfortunately, we know that media attention equals donor attention. And when the media is done, the cameras move on to the next crisis."

In the case of IsraAID, they know that the needs are still there, particularly around trauma, mental health, and infrastructure. And so, they stay on average five years after a disaster to provide ongoing support. They spend that time building a local team, with some Israeli international experts, and train them in different fields of expertise, depending on the need. Then they support them for a few years through implementation and until they are self-sufficient.

That's the goal, Yotam says emphatically, "To be first on the ground, but even more important, last to leave. First in, last out."

Yotam's Postscript

IsraAID's vision is to be the humanitarian wing of the Startup-Nation. When the organization was founded 2001, the goal was to respond to crises and bring Israeli expertise to the most vulnerable countries. On October 7, 2023, the worst disaster of our lifetime struck at home. By October 8, we launched a large-scale humanitarian operation in Israel, something we never thought we would do. We took the skills and capabilities gained over the past 23 years from working in 64 countries. We drew on expertise gained from working in refugee camps and with hundreds of thousands of displaced people to help those who suffered the most—the community members of Kibbutz Be'eri, the Nova music festival survivors, and members of unrecognized Bedouin communities in southern Israel who didn't have saferooms or rocket shelters to protect them from the thousands of rockets fired from Gaza. Just like in every place that we work, we will continue to assist for as long as we are needed to help survivors rebuild their lives. We recognize and are ready for this most important task of our lifetime.

"You can't just yell at problems."
"I came in with my science and my data,
but I forgot the human dimension."

—Tomer Malchi

CultivAid

If Israelis have a reputation for not accepting no, Tomer Malchi is the personification of Israeli-ness.

He spent his earliest years on Moshav Avichail before his family moved to Monsey, New York. The Malchi home reverberated with Mizrachi music, and a large collection of palm-shaped amulets known as hamsas decorated the walls. The family's small locksmith business struggled to compete with the large chain stores, which instilled in Tomer a lifelong resolve to fight for the underdog. In his twenties, long before Starbucks organizing campaigns made front-page news, Tomer was working as a barista in a Manhattan Starbucks and as a union organizer demanding better conditions and pay for himself and his colleagues.

While preparing coffees on shift one day, he looked up to see a girl in line making a face at him. "So, I made a face back," he says with a chuckle. "I heard her speaking in Hebrew, so when she got to the front of the line, we started chatting in Hebrew, and I found out her name was Shira. And then, you know how it goes, I gave her free drinks. She came back for free drinks." He smiles at the memory. "I asked her for her number, and she said no. I kept asking, and eventually she agreed." The two eventually moved back to Israel and married.

Professionally, Tomer was ready for a change. While he was committed to fighting injustice, he wanted to find better solutions for doing so. "You can't just yell at problems," he says. "I wanted to find a more methodical and data-driven approach to getting things done." He had developed an interest in water sciences, and he spent hours in Barnes & Noble stores around Manhattan reading everything he could on the topic. When he and Shira returned to Israel, he enrolled in the Hebrew University's Faculty of Agriculture to complete a second bachelor's degree, followed by a master's degree, followed by a PhD in soil and water sciences.

Eager to put his theoretical learnings into practice, he helped establish an Israeli branch of Engineers Without Borders. His first project was a disaster. The plan had been to build a green space, using wastewater treatment in the Kidron Basin of East Jerusalem. Tomer devoted himself to the project, spending dozens of hours thinking through technical details and intricacies of wastewater treatment and biogas production. "The project failed," he says bluntly and without the least bit of embarrassment. "And the reason it failed is that we didn't spend enough time talking to the locals who would have to live with the project. I kept trying to make it work, until an older Palestinian woman said to me, 'Why would I let any Jewish person build on my property?' And when she said that, I knew it was over. I came in with my science and my data, but I forgot the human dimension."

Fortunately, Tomer is not easily deterred. He is relentlessly optimistic and finds lessons in each failure. That said, listening to his stories, one gets the sense that Tomer almost insists on pursuing the most difficult paths.

In 2013, he learned that two Israeli friends named Ben and Moti, while working in Ethiopia, had begun to build a primary school in partnership with the local community. Before the school construction was finished, the company they were working for ceased operations, and so they returned to Israel. Ben and Moti wondered if Engineers Without Borders could help finish the project. Sensing an adventure, Tomer outlined a plan to complete construction of the school and to build a water treatment system and agricultural fields that would see the school become self-sustaining.

The three Israelis managed to raise $25,000 for the project. They arrived in Waarree Village, a few hours south of Harar, and having learned a valuable lesson from the wastewater treatment project, spent days talking to local villagers about the project plans. Before construction could resume, they learned that the company's new owners objected to having former employees on-site. The company's management went so far as to have government officials threaten to make arrests if Tomer and his friends didn't abandon the project.

The young Israelis pleaded with the regional government to appeal the decision, until they received permission to proceed. Elated, they purchased equipment, transported it to the site, and resumed work on the school. Before long, the regional government reversed its decision, and they were once again threatened with halting operations or facing imprisonment. Recognizing the seriousness of the new directive, they fled the region.

Most people would give up at this point, but Tomer continued looking for a work-around. He approached Dr. Taddele Hagos, director of the Tigray Development Association, and asked for his help navigating the politics. Dr. Hagos had a different idea and invited the Israelis to work at the Kallamino High School in Mekelle. The Israelis turned him down, and they spent another six months trying to get approval for the first project. Finding no path forward, they returned to Dr. Hagos and accepted his offer.

The new project was the start of a new chapter. Tomer and his friends assembled a team to set up a two-acre demonstration and training farm that introduced Israeli agricultural technologies to the region, including a drip irrigation system and hybrid seeds. Israeli volunteers ran demonstrations on the farm, and the results spoke for themselves. The yields were ten times the size of what the local farmers were producing.

Impressed by the young Israeli team, the Tigray Development Association asked them to upgrade the entire farm at Kallamino. They introduced ten hectares of pressurized drip irrigation, a greenhouse to raise seedlings, and the first drip-irrigated avocado orchard in Ethiopia. The site attracted agriculturalists from across the region, eager to learn from the Israeli team. Tomer and his partners also introduced open days for farmers in the region to learn about the techniques employed at Kallamino. At the first open day, Tomer was approached by a man named Alem, who became instantly memorable because he spoke English with a Swedish accent, despite never having set foot outside Ethiopia. Alem had arrived with a request for spare faucets, but the odd request was forgotten amidst the excitement of the day.

At the next open day, Alem appeared once again and asked Tomer for spare faucets. This time Tomer wanted to learn his story. He found out that Alem and his brother, Yemane, had founded Elshadai Children's Village for orphans of the Ethiopian-Eritrean war. The home looks after four hundred orphans and operates a farm, dairy barn, and school on the outskirts of Wukro in Tigray region. Intrigued, Tomer visited the village and learned that Alem was a self-taught farmer running an impressive fifty-acre farm. Tomer contacted MASHAV to help set up a vegetable demonstration site, an avocado orchard, farm equipment, and eventually an apple orchard. Tomer and his team visited on a weekly basis to consult and provide technical support to local farmers. Before long, Alem's farm went from generating 25 percent of the funds needed to run the school to generating enough revenue to make the village entirely self-sustaining.

Word of their success spread, and in 2016, officials from the Ethiopian Ministry of Health invited Tomer's team to assist in developing an implementation plan for the Seqota Declaration. An initiative of the Ethiopian government, the declaration aimed to end child malnutrition by 2030. The town of Seqota had been the epicenter of a catastrophic famine in the 1980s. Hunger has continued to plague Africa's second most populous country. Ethiopia is home to nearly 105 million people, almost all of whom rely on rain-fed agriculture and livestock for the food and income they need to survive. The reliance on agriculture leaves families vulnerable to hunger when droughts, flash floods, poverty, and conflict throw millions of people into crisis. According to USAID, malnutrition contributes to more than 50 percent of all infant and child deaths in Ethiopia.[58]

Tomer and his partners were still graduate students when they were invited to join the government committee, alongside experts with twenty or thirty years of experience. Undaunted, they were eager to share their perspective on how Israeli agricultural and water technologies could help battle malnutrition. The government brought them on as technical consultants to support a range of programs and studies.

---

[58] USAID, *Ethiopia: Nutrition,* https://www.usaid.gov/ethiopia/nutrition.

It soon became clear that this new work demanded full-time attention and resources, so Tomer and his friends founded CultivAid to introduce Israeli agricultural technology and know-how to East African communities. Aiming to have a sizable and scalable impact, they focused on training and capacity-building. CultivAid assessed a wide array of vegetables and fruits to determine which were most appropriate for the agro-ecology of the region, then established protocols for precise irrigation and fertilizer application. They built a series of agricultural demonstration and research farms that became hubs for farmers and agriculturalists to learn, purchase supplies, and sell produce. Graduates of Israeli agricultural schools were invited to spend six months in Ethiopia running the demonstration farms and training locals.

Broadening the training programs, CultivAid set up training centers in Ethiopia's agricultural universities, where the course load had been heavily academic with little practical skill development. "In theory, they know how an irrigation system works," Tomer explains, "but during their studies they aren't ever given the chance to touch or try one." CultivAid brought the equipment to the students and gave them the chance to try them out.

As technical consultants to the Seqota Declaration, CultivAid developed the technical designs for two R&D sites in Amhara and Tigray, and agricultural training centers at Gondar and Axsum universities. The R&D sites follow the Israeli model of using data to optimize decision-making.

"Farmers should ideally know how much water is being consumed on their farm, be it groundwater or rainwater," Tomer says. "They should have information on weather patterns and the chemical composition of the soil. And they should have market information to know which crops are in higher demand and will be more profitable, plus nutritional data for the local community, to identify dietary needs and nutritional deficiencies." When this information is available, farmers make informed decisions about what to grow during different times of the year.

CultivAid has expanded its work in East Africa, establishing more than twenty agricultural programs and launching dozens of projects to offer solutions to fundamental challenges in the agriculture and water sectors. The organization's Agricultural Innovation and Technology Centers (AITEC) model combines commercial farming with local ownership, Israeli training and technology, and smallholder extension services. These centers have proven to be a successful means by which thousands of local smallholders can engage within an ecosystem that exposes them to commercial operations and provides them access to tools, inputs, and training.

In 2020, a series of devastating catastrophes struck Ethiopia. A locust outbreak in the north devastated crops, COVID-19 struck the country, and there was an outbreak in violence between the federal government and regional government of Tigray, which led to a massive humanitarian catastrophe. A population of 5.2 million people in Ethiopia's northern region faced hunger and lacked access to basic supplies, after the government imposed a blockade and violence hampered aid delivery.

When violence erupted, CultivAid's staff on the ground found themselves in a war zone. With roads closed and cell phones not working, the team in Israel went days without hearing from their eight local agronomists and four Israeli Interns.

"It was the most stressful thing I've ever experienced," Tomer tells me. "We did everything we could to locate the Israelis, working with government agencies and the Red Cross. We finally managed to contact locals who owned satellite phones, so we would record messages in Hebrew with instructions." It sometimes took two or three days for the locals to find their way to the Israelis and play the messages. After a few frightening weeks, the Israelis were able to leave Tigray as part of an international caravan, to Tomer's enormous relief. "I was glad that we got them out safely, but we had to leave behind our local staff. And they aren't just staff. We've known them for years. They are our family."

The war dragged on, and while most NGOs stopped operating, CultivAid continued its work and even set up a program to support internally displaced people through agricultural training and access to seeds. During the first year of the conflict, over one million seedlings were distributed to farmers. In late 2022, a peace agreement ended the war in Tigray, but millions more people were left trapped in poverty and hunger. Tomer returned to reestablish operations, working with partners on the ground to revitalize the agricultural markets.

Despite the setbacks, Tomer's confidence isn't shaken. Just the opposite, in fact. "Africa is rising. Investments are being made. A transformation is happening, and it will happen with or without us. We plan to be a part of it by getting more Israeli technology into the hands of African farmers."

Tomer's Postscript

Following the attacks on October 7, CultivAid staff were devastated to learn that friends and colleagues were taken hostage by terrorists to Gaza. In the weeks that followed, key Israeli staff based in Ethiopia, Tanzania, Kenya, and Israel were called to reserve duty in the IDF. Operations were disrupted but not halted. With a heavy heart, the remaining staff continued in their mission, believing that it was even more important to build relationships and demonstrate Israel's desire to share knowledge and solve global challenges together.

* * *

"We came to have a real relationship.
They knew I cared about them."

—Gili Navon

Amar Majuli

Gili Navon grew up listening to stories from her grandfather about his years in the Palmach, the underground army of the Yishuv (the pre-state Jewish community) during the period of the British Mandate. They were stories of daring and courage, of smuggling Jewish refugees into the country in defiance of the British immigration laws. She often wondered if her own life would be marked by such a sense of purpose.

Following her army service, Gili took her big trip to India and spent a year traveling through Varanasi, Ladakh, and Kerala, studying yoga and learning Sanskrit. It didn't take long for her to fall in love with the country, its people, rich traditions, and diverse cultures. She returned to Israel in 2007 to study anthropology and sociology at the Hebrew University of Jerusalem. After graduation, she returned to India and continued traversing the country, preferring to spend time in quieter areas far from tourists. In India's far northeast, she found a remote river island in Assam state called Majuli, near the borders of Myanmar, Bangladesh, and China. Accessible by ferry, the island is encircled by the rushing waters of the Brahmaputra River. With a population of around 170,000 people, residents of the island are mainly tribals from different communities, including the Mising tribe, the Sonowal, the Kacharis, the Deoris, and the Ahoms.

In Majuli, Gili thought she had found paradise. She accompanied locals to the jungle to pick herbs and helped with household chores. She watched them spin raw silk and cotton into colorful garments. She worked to learn the local language so she could communicate directly with them. She saw the struggle for sustenance in this low-caste, subsistence-farming society where tourists rarely venture. "In Majuli I met a completely different way of life and a kind of poverty I had never seen in Israel," Gili reports. "There is discrimination, social exclusion, a lack of opportunities. Added to this, most people lack financial security, especially women."

The island was once the world's biggest river island, but it is slowly being washed away by the fast-moving waters of the Brahmaputra River. Gili heard from locals about how erosion rips at Majuli's banks every year, sweeping away homes and submerging lands. During the monsoon season, parts of the island flood. In the last fifty years, Majuli has lost 50 percent of its land. The majority of the island's residents are dependent on agriculture, and as the years pass, this loss of land is taking its toll and exacerbating the cycle of poverty.

After eight months in Majuli, Gili returned to Israel, but her thoughts remained with the island. Seeking a way to help, she enrolled in Hebrew University of Jerusalem's Glocal (a blend of the words "global" and "local") Community Development Studies master's degree program. The program requires each student to complete a four-month internship in a disadvantaged community, and naturally Gili chose Majuli. She struggled to find a local NGO that would serve as her official sponsor, and after finally finding one and convincing Hebrew University of its validity, she bought a ticket to India, not entirely sure that it did in fact exist.

Once in Majuli, she met up with representatives of the NGO and was assigned to evaluate a project that had been running for four years and was supposed to provide income for members of the Mising Tribe through traditional weaving projects. Gili was in her element traveling through villages and talking with locals. It helped that she spoke Hindi and Sanskrit. The results of the evaluation were disappointing. Years of investment in workshops and training hadn't translated to improved livelihoods for residents of Majuli. Gili considered the findings and thought about the people she had met. Many of them were talented women, proud of their tradition and motivated to work hard. She felt confident that given the right opportunities, they could better support their families and even grow some savings.

Two of the main challenges were that the weavers didn't have access to larger markets and that they also lacked access to financing. At the same time, social discrimination meant women weren't being given opportunities to make decisions about the work. The challenges were compounded by the remoteness of Majuli, its harsh weather cycles, and basic living conditions. Gili had spent months interviewing women, and she identified twenty-four talented weavers with big personalities whom she thought had leadership potential.

Together, they began the arduous task of forming a weaving cooperative to turn their cultural tradition into a viable source of income. The goal was to give the women ownership of the business and the ability to direct their own futures. None of the women, including Gili, knew how to form a legal cooperative, but Gili was determined, and being Israeli, she was unrelenting. Gili visited the local cooperative office and convinced the staff to run a workshop to teach Majuli women how to navigate the long processes and bureaucracies. Gili encouraged local women to learn about and run every dimension of the business, from filing the paperwork to opening a bank account to identifying new markets that cut out the middlemen to electing their own leadership.

The women chose the name "Rengam" for the cooperative, which is Mising for "a united group." They identified new market opportunities in Guwahati, a city on the mainland with a population of over one million people and a high demand for traditionally woven goods. In time, the women strengthened their identity and developed pride in their tradition and tribe. Gili is a fervent believer in an assets-based-for-community-development (ABCD) approach to international development. Rather than focusing on the problems and needs of a community, she identifies and builds on its existing strengths and assets. In Majuli, she believes the women were the greatest asset.

After four months, Gili returned to Israel to complete her master's program and graduate. She found work in a high-tech company but stayed in close contact with her friends back in Majuli. Feeling unsettled, she went to interview for a different job and during the interview spoke passionately about her work and experiences in India. Rather than receive a job offer, she was stunned when the prospective employer offered her $10,000 to return to Majuli and continue her work. Gili called her friend and fellow Glocal alumnus, Shaked, to share the good news. Shaked's response was, "I'm coming with you."

Gili and Shaked partnered with locals in Majuli to establish Amar Majuli ("Our Majuli"), a nonprofit whose mission is to provide partners and their families with sustainable livelihoods while gaining leadership skills. The heart of Amar Majuli's work remained the Rengam Women Weavers Cooperative, but Gili and Shaked searched for ways to empower and inspire the women. They arranged to take a group of local weavers to the mainland to visit a larger cooperative and learn from other tribes. For many of the women, it was their first time leaving the island, and it became a turning point in helping expand their notions of what is possible. Gili suggested that the women of Rengam weave new products that would appeal to tourists and Western markets, such as scarves, table runners, and yoga bags. The new items were a hit. Little by little, Rengam expanded the work to fifteen villages with over two hundred weavers.

Majuli's villages are far from critical infrastructure, such as markets and hospitals. Public transportation isn't reliable, and women traditionally don't drive cars. Since Majuli is flat, cycling offers an easy solution, in an economically sustainable model. So, to enhance the mobility and independence for community members, Amar Majuli set up two bicycle banks in remote villages. The bicycle banks work like a car loan. Each month, a woman pays a few pennies to use a bike, and by the end of the year, she will have paid in enough to own it outright and gain freedom of mobility in the process. Amar Majuli even ran bicycle workshops to teach local women how to ride.

One project led to another. Gili convinced Netafim to donate drip irrigation tubes for small-scale farmers. This led to the development of a sustainable agriculture program in cooperation with the Farm2Food Foundation. The program provides tools for poor farmers—both men and women—to increase sustainable agro-economic productivity alongside traditional knowledge and a focus on organic agriculture.

During the monsoon season, when the island suffers from floods, Amar Majuli shifts into relief mode, organizing medical clinics, distributing water filters, and delivering food items to people whose homes flood. "This is a very hard period of the year," Gili explains. "Roads are blocked, there are shortages of drinking water, sanitation gets backed up, and people get sick but can't access medical services."

As the years have passed, Shaked and Gili have slowly stepped back and encouraged locals from Majuli to step into leadership and decision-making roles. They encourage women and youth to identify local needs, such as much-needed repairs to the home of a senior before the rainy season, fixing a road, or replacing a water tank.

Today, Amar Majuli's executive committee is run by locals from Majuli. Through Rengam and other projects, they are building a livelihood with dignity. The experience has changed how they see themselves and their potential. Ten years after the organization was founded, the weaving cooperative counts about two hundred women from seventeen villages providing livelihoods for almost five hundred families. There is even a physical center designed to showcase the artisan's handicrafts and a place for visitors to meet weavers.

Gili is back in Israel raising three young boys who keep her busy, but she stays in touch with the local staff and board members of Majuli and serves as a thought partner and fundraiser from afar. "Today if you speak to the people on the ground in

Majuli, they may or may not mention me when they tell their story," Gili concludes. "I see that as a great success. It's their organization; they feel ownership. It's now their story."

Gili's Postscript

One day after the October 7 attack, my family and I evacuated from our home in Tziv'on, which is located 4km from Israel's northern border with Lebanon. Along with about twenty other community members, we temporarily related to Neot Semadar which is a 45-minute drive from Eilat, Israel's southernmost city.

We went from living in the green mountains of northern Israel to living in the parched desert of southern Israel. I also went from assisting people who were evacuated from their homes to being an evacuee myself.

There is a tremendous amount of grief, disbelief, and helplessness to try to overcome. I cope by taking all that I have learned over the years to assist other evacuees and ensure that we have everything we need, from housing to education, to emotional and physical support. At the same time, I am doing all that I can to assist the women in the Rengam Tribal Weaver's Cooperative expand their operations, build operational capacity, and empower their leadership. At a time when it seems like everything has been destroyed, I am driven to be a builder. It's who I am.

"We send hundreds of thousands of Israelis to the poorest countries, so let's leverage the fact that they are going anyway and let's turn Israel into a global power of charity."

—Gili Cohen

Heroes for Life

With so many Israelis traveling through low-income countries each year, Gili Cohen wondered if he could harness that spirit of adventure into volunteerism.

Gili grew up in Beit Shemesh, a town near Jerusalem, to parents who were devoted to Israel. Their own families had immigrated to Israel from Yazd, Iran, when Israel was still a young state. The family delights in telling the story of Gili's great grandfather, who traveled on a donkey from Yazd to Hebron's Tomb of the Patriarchs and Matriarchs, just to spend three days praying at the holy site, before making the arduous return trip to his home in Iran.

Israel had long been central to the dreams of both families. When the Jewish Agency offered Iranian Jews the chance to immigrate to Israel, Gili's grandfather accepted the offer but refused to accept any money and instead paid for his family's tickets and that of thirty others from their village. When they arrived, Gili's father's family settled in Jerusalem, while his mother's family, who had been one of Yazd's poorer families, was placed in an immigrant absorption camp (ma'abara) alongside other new immigrants from Iran, Morocco, and Romania. It was the period of the *tzena*, or austerity measures, when goods were strictly rationed.

Given the economic hardships of the time, even his father's relatively well-to-do family didn't have enough food. Even so, whenever the family prepared rice, they set aside a portion for people with even less. "*Chesed* was central to how I was raised," Gili tells me. "My brothers and sister and I were always taught to think about others and their needs." While he was growing up, his parents ran the local bookstore and also ran a free loan society, which allowed struggling families to borrow books for the year and then return them when the school year was over.

After high school, Gili served for a decade in the Israeli military, rising to become a team commander of the elite Duvdevan counterterrorism unit. *Duvdevan* is the Hebrew word for cherry, and the name comes from the belief that the cream always rises to the top, and the only thing that goes on top of the cream is a cherry. This special unit conducts high-risk undercover operations in Arab territories. The level of preparedness and risk deeply influenced Gili's outlook toward life.

"To go undercover is complicated and dangerous in places like the West Bank. In my case, I had to speak fluent Arabic. If you make a small mistake, it means you won't come back to your family." But it was good training for his later life. "After doing this for ten years and conducting hundreds of operations in the West Bank and Gaza Strip, other things, like how to bring a group of Israelis to India, seem pretty easy to figure out. If there is something huge that I got from my military service, it's that I can figure anything out."

The relentless danger and long hours of army life were a constant strain on his wife, Rachel, and their young daughter. "I was called to the unit at all hours of the day and night, and one day Rachel finally said to me: 'I love you and I love the army, but it's too much because your daughter doesn't know you when you come home. She sees you and she runs away.'"

Gili knew his wife was right, and while they discussed what their future could look like, he said to her, "Let's go to the travel agency and buy an air ticket to the Far East. Each time I need to leave on short notice, the ticket will be on the fridge, and we can look at it and know that in a few months we'll be traveling together." Rachel agreed, and together they began planning their own big trip. Gili suggested that they should travel for four months, leaving their baby with her grandmother, but Rachel's response was, "Are you crazy? I won't leave her for more than two weeks." They debated and negotiated, "and like every negotiation in our relationship," Gili says, "we decided to compromise. So, we went for two and a half weeks. And that was one of my more successful negotiations."

In 2013, the young couple departed for Thailand. It was just the time and escape they needed together. On their travels, they felt connections to home wherever they went. In Chiang Mai, a city in the mountainous northern region, he saw street signs in Thai, English, and Hebrew. On Samui Island, they found a Chabad House for Friday dinner. So many people attended that the meal took place in a room that seated seven hundred people, and since that still wasn't enough space, a dinner was held every forty-five minutes to accommodate the Israelis and Jewish tourists looking for a traditional Shabbat meal.

Gili was struck by the notion that this one small, remote island had thousands of visiting Israelis. He then thought about the tens of thousands of Israelis that were, at that moment, in Bangkok, India, Nepal, Chile, Peru, and beyond. "I thought to myself: the Jewish state has a purpose to be a light unto the nations. We send hundreds of thousands of Israelis to the poorest countries, so let's leverage the fact that they are going anyway, and let's turn Israel into a global power of charity and chesed."

That thought motivated him to establish Heroes for Life. The idea was for the organization to give young Israelis a meaningful volunteer opportunity and show the world the compassionate face of Israel. He set a goal to have an organization operating in twenty countries within ten years. It was a big dream, complicated by the fact that Gili was still in the army and didn't know the first thing about starting a nonprofit. In line to become a senior commander in Duvdevan, he was torn between running Heroes for Life and continuing his career in the military.

Gili took the dilemma to his unit commander, who offered an idea. He suggested that Gili pursue a degree, which the army would pay, along with a monthly salary, and at the same time he could work on turning his idea into a reality. After he graduated, they would reevaluate. Relieved, Gili decided to study law and turned his mind to recruiting and running his first delegation.

"It was so complicated," he admits. "I didn't know how to connect to the Israeli Foreign Ministry, who to call, or what to say." On Shabbat afternoon, he was sitting with his father, explaining the challenges, when his father said, "Gili, Israel's consul general to Mumbai lives three doors away. Go knock on his door and speak with Danny." He did just that and walked down the street to knock on the door of Daniel Sivan.

"He opened the door wearing a tank top and shorts, looked at me, and said, 'Hello, Moti's son—I remember you when you were just a little boy.' At that moment, I knew it was going to work out."

Gili explained his vision, and Danny told him, "Listen, I finished my posting in Mumbai two months ago, but call my deputy, Matan Zamir, tell him Danny Sivan sent you. He will help you."

That is how Heroes for Life chose Mumbai as the destination for their first delegation. Matan promised to find volunteer sites and pay for accommodations. Gili realized he'd need to raise funds to cover the other costs. His father donated 1,000 NIS, a sizable sum of money for him but not nearly enough to fund a delegation.

Gili and his wife had saved by 3,000 NIS for a vacation. She instructed him to use the money to take an advance trip to Mumbai and arrange the details for his first delegation. He had just enough to fly to Mumbai for forty-eight hours to make the arrangements and visit the volunteer sites.

The next challenge was finding volunteers to participate in the program. Gili set up a Facebook page, which was slow to gain any traction. One day, while visiting a friend in the army who commanded a unit, his friend had an idea. They collected the cell phones of every young recruit and sent invitations to all their friends to "like" the Heroes for Life Facebook page. The strategy drew a lot of attention to the page, and twelve people signed up to join the first volunteer mission.

Participants were asked to pay for their own flight and medical insurance, the consulate covered accommodations and security, and Gili's father found a supplier to donate two hundred meals of freeze-dried kosher shawarma that they could smother in Indian spices.

The first group, like every subsequent group of volunteers, spent half of their day working in schools teaching subjects selected by the head of the school. It could be English, math, geography, but no matter the topic, the Israeli volunteers took the strategy employed by Israeli schools to make the lessons highly interactive. English is taught through songs, math through games that have the children running to search for numbers and combinations. The other half of the day is dedicated to projects like painting and fixing schools and homes, renovating orphanages, and even building new rooms for the local school, with the help of a local construction engineer.

With a successful proof of concept under his belt, Gili was able to raise funds and send a delegation to Argentina. They sent a prominent photojournalist along with the delegation, and his newspaper article drew a lot of attention. Since then, there have been more applicants than available spots on delegations.

Heroes for Life has expanded its operations to new communities working in partnership with the local ministry of education. The delegations always include at least a few people fluent in the native language of their destination. Medical professionals, such as dentists, join the group if requested by the local community. As large and successful as the organization has become, they have retained symbolic legacies from their earliest days. Even now, the staff must pay for their first air ticket, because as Gili says, "I had to. So, they should."

Today, Heroes for Life has three full-time staff and a lot of volunteers helping run the organization. They operate in sixteen countries, send around sixteen delegations abroad every year, and have fourteen hundred volunteer alumni who worked with over seventeen thousand children. The program is so popular that in the last five years, more than twenty-five thousand Israelis signed up to join a delegation. Gili has devised the "30-30 plan" that would see him sending out thirty delegations per year to thirty countries by 2030.

Gili has tapped into the energy of thousands of traveling young Israelis, adding an additional dimension of meaning to their trips and giving countless communities around the globe the chance to see the spirit of Israelis. Still connected to his roots in the army, each delegation is named for an Israeli who fell during his or her service to the country, a gesture that means so much to their families.

"I didn't come up with the idea to change the world," Gili says. "I had the idea to innovate, and change has followed."

CONCLUSION

"Our hope, the two-thousand-year-old hope, will not be lost."

—"Hatikva," Israel's national anthem

David Ben-Gurion first set eyes on Sde Boker, a kibbutz nestled in the heart of the Negev Desert, at the age of sixty-seven. It was not long after the kibbutz was founded by ten young men and two young women in 1952 when the then-prime minister was driving past and saw the community's young members at work. He stepped out of his car and asked the young people why they had chosen to settle in this place with its harsh conditions and unforgiving heat. They replied that the Nabateans had lived there two thousand years ago, so why couldn't they? So impressed was Ben-Gurion with their resolve that he decided to join them.

When he retired from politics, he left his home in Tel Aviv and, along with his wife Paula, joined the kibbutz. They lived in a wooden cottage with a large study that held one thousand volumes of books. Ben-Gurion agreed to work four hours a day in the kibbutz but quickly realized that the hard physical labor was too much for his advanced years. Instead, he helped as a sheepshearer. While returning to office in 1955 required him to spend most of his time in the center of Israel, following his final retirement in 1963 he returned to his home in the desert and stayed until he died in 1973.

When people asked why he moved to the simple, scorching-hot, rural community, he answered, "I came here because I knew everything had to be created from the beginning, and now I intend to stay here."[59] Few people understood better than Ben-Gurion how to see past what was in front of him to the potential beyond. When he looked out over the rocky, scrubby hills of the Negev, he didn't see a desert wasteland. He saw bustling and expansive cities that would one day answer the national challenge of absorbing the huge influx of immigrants and dispersing the population throughout the country. And he decided that he would be a part of building that next story of Israel. A speech he gave in 1955 offers a glimpse into his vision:

> It is in the Negev that the creativity and pioneer vigor of Israel will be tested, and this will be a crucial test. Israel's capacity for science and research will be tested in the Negev and it is incumbent upon our scientists and researchers to focus on new areas of research which residents of the North will have need of: research to desalinate seawater with inexpensive processes; to exploit solar energy which is so abundant in our country, and especially in the Negev; to use wind power to generate electric power; to prevent the wastage of scarce rain water which flows unused to the Mediterranean or to the Dead Sea; to build ponds across the length and

[59] Granger Blair, "Visit with Ben-Gurion in the Desert," *New York Times*, January 12, 1964.

> breadth of the Negev for collecting precious rainwater, to investigate the vegetation found in the Negev, despite its aridity.... [I]t is incumbent upon Israel's scientists to reveal the secrets of nature that are unique to our land...."[60]

As I write this, I am in Israel celebrating the seventy-fifth anniversary of the state's founding. Traversing the country, I try to imagine the state as it was in its earliest days. Israel at seventy-five, with its expansive highways, high-rises, and high-tech sector, would be unrecognizable to its founders and early citizens.

The birth of a modern Jewish state fundamentally changed the condition of the Jewish people. It offered a shield of security and sovereignty against the murderous designs and painful indifference that characterized too much of Jewish history. The pioneers of Zionism understood that a Jewish state in the Jews' ancestral homeland was essential for a people who inevitably became scapegoats and the targets of hatred wherever they lived. Zionism is the dream, and Israel is that dream come to life. Here at last was a place on earth where Jews could assume responsibility for their own security. The aspirations for this state were grounded in both Jewish and universal principles, as made clear by the state's founding document, the Declaration of Independence:

> The State of Israel will be open for Jewish immigration and for the Ingathering of the Exiles; it will foster the development of the country for the benefit of all its inhabitants; it

[60] David Ben-Gurion, speech, "Significance of the Negev," January 1955.

> will be based on freedom, justice and peace as envisaged by the prophets of Israel; it will ensure complete equality of social and political rights to all its inhabitants irrespective of religion, race or sex; it will guarantee freedom of religion, conscience, language, education and culture; it will safeguard the Holy Places of all religions; and it will be faithful to the principles of the Charter of the United Nations.

Out of 193 countries in the world, there would be one state, comprising just 0.1 percent of the land area on earth, with a distinctly Jewish character. Just one country in sync with the Jewish calendar and its Jewish holidays. Where Jewish music, literature, and theater would be elevated and celebrated. Where the language and currency of ancient Israel would be given new life. Where the parliament, named the Knesset, would take its name and fix its membership at 120 after the Knesset Hagedolah (Great Assembly), the representative Jewish council convened in Jerusalem in the fifth century BCE.

Judaism is a religion, an ethnicity, a culture, and a people, all of which is interwoven with the fundamental essence of the Jewish state. In Israel, you can walk in the places where the patriarchs and matriarchs—Abraham, Sarah, Isaac, Rebekah, Jacob, Leah, and Rachel—walked. Every Friday, Shabbat candle-lighting times are printed on the front page of the newspaper. Streets are named for Jewish luminaries like King David, Queen Esther, Ibn Ezra, Hayyim Nahman Bialik, Shai Agnon, Theodor Herzl, and, of course, Golda Meir. In Israel, the glue on envelopes and stamps is kosher. Stores sell gourmet jelly donuts for Hannukah and hummus-flavored ice cream all year round. During the holiday of Purim, children dress up as Marvel superheroes but also as Jewish superheroes, like Queen Esther and Judah the Maccabee. Public buses have signs that encourage courtesy by quoting the Biblical passage, "You shall rise before the aged and show deference to the old." Those same buses display signs reading *Chag Sameach* (Happy Holidays) ahead of Jewish holidays.

The casual vibrancy of Jewish life that characterizes Israel today was unimaginable to centuries of Jews who lived in exile, and even for the state's pioneers. Their goal was survival. Wars of annihilation directed by professional and well-funded Arab armies, diplomatic and economic sanctions that created international isolation, the influx of traumatized and penniless refugees, rampant unemployment, chronic food and water shortages threatened the very survival of the nascent state. Taken together, the threats seemed insurmountable. But as Golda Meir told freshman Senator Joe Biden in 1973, "We Israelis have a secret weapon. We have nowhere else to go."

Resilience, determination, and innovation characterized those early years of hardship. As each crisis receded, Israelis turned their determined efforts to the work of state-building, innovating in the fields of security, agriculture, health care, infrastructure, education, arts, and social welfare. Despite the small population and lack of natural resources, the country's leaders had big ambitions. Ingenuity and entrepreneurship were celebrated. Chutzpah took root as a national ethos. As time passed, the country's confidence grew, and its citizens turned outward. They shared their success with other countries confronting similar challenges. With each passing decade, as Israel grew more secure and prosperous, it became a model and inspiration to developing nations that sought to achieve the same transformation.

Today, Israel is nicknamed the "Start-Up Nation," and it is celebrated for its booming economy and ingenious innovations. Less celebrated is the story of how Israel lifted up other nations as it lifted up itself—the story of Israel, a force for good in the world.

David Ben-Gurion and Golda Meir spoke and wrote openly about their motivations for founding MASHAV, Israel's Agency for International Development Cooperation. They believed that Israel had a moral obligation to share its knowledge and expertise with other countries. At the same time, they saw development cooperation as a route to tangibly boost Israel's global standing and to promote peace, security, and prosperity between nations. It was a dual mission of idealism and pragmatism. MASHAV became a leading player in the field of international development cooperation and was celebrated for its impact.

For a while, the agency enjoyed strong political support and was a source of great pride to the Israeli people. The wars of 1967 and 1973 recast alliances and cast a dark shadow over Israel's work in developing nations. As relations between nations deteriorated, so too did the political will and public support for Israel's international development agenda. It has never reemerged as a government priority, and today Israel spends far less on international aid than the OECD standard.

Even so, the ideals that gave birth to Israel's overseas partnerships remain ingrained in the state's DNA. The Israeli international development nongovernmental sector has grown exponentially in the last thirty years. Israeli NGOs are working all over the world to provide humanitarian aid and relief services to people affected by natural disasters, armed conflicts, and other crises.

Israel's critics have cynically accused these organizations of "rubble-washing." They dismiss the work abroad as self-interested public relations efforts that are meant to deflect from Israel's conflict with the Palestinians. The mendacious charges ignore Israel's long-standing work in international development and emergency relief, and the self-described motivations of the individuals involved, which very often are rooted in Jewish principles to help others in need. More often than not, the criticisms come from groups and individuals who look for any reason to undermine Israel's legitimacy. While Israel has both domestic and foreign challenges, to be sure, these struggles don't negate its efforts in international development or make them any less laudable.

Changing times have also seen people call into question the ethical grounds of professional international development work. While there is always room for improvement, the individuals and organizations profiled in this book are all committed to providing aid to all people in need, regardless of their ethnicity, religion, or political affiliation. They work closely with local communities and governments to ensure that their assistance is designed and delivered sensitively and appropriately, with the highest professional and ethical standards. They share the goal of empowering their partners to be self-reliant and self-sustaining. Thanks to them, pockets of this planet are a little safer, a little healthier, and a little more economically secure.

Nations are influenced by a variety of factors, including political, economic, and social considerations. While it is possible that countries receiving aid and support from Israel may be open to being more supportive of Israel at the United Nations, there is no clear evidence that this is the case. Israel's Foreign Ministry does not instruct its ambassadors to make aid contingent on political support in international forums, though it may opt to work with friendly nations when considering new sustainable development projects (this is not the case when it comes to emergency relief and humanitarian crises, as evidenced by examples in this book). Moreover, Israel's work in low-income countries rarely draws the attention of international journalists or influences global public opinion.

Despite the lack of political reciprocity or improved reputation, the work continues to expand for the simple reason that Israelis feel compelled to help. Whether the driver be idealism, pragmatism, adventurism, chutzpah-ism, or some combination, the Israelis who have devoted their careers to elevating low-income nations prove that, like Israel, you can be small and make a big impact. In an age where cynicism reigns, they inspire us to think big, dream audaciously, act boldly, and work tirelessly to build a better future for ourselves and for others.

ABOUT THE AUTHOR

Aviva Klompas is co-founder and CEO of Boundless, a think-action tank focused on Israel and antisemitism. Previously, she served as the Director of Speechwriting for Israel's delegation to the United Nations in New York City and as a Senior Policy Advisor in Ontario Cabinet Office.

A leading thinker on Israel, Zionism, and antisemitism, Aviva is frequently invited to address audiences all over the world. Her work has appeared in the *New York Times*, the *Wall Street Journal*, *Newsweek*, the *Jerusalem Post*, and other international publications. Aviva's debut memoir, *Speaking for Israel*, offers an insider's glimpse into diplomatic life on the global stage.

Printed in Great Britain
by Amazon

47729973R00136